THROUGH A GLASS DARKLY

Readings on the
Concept of God

EDITED AND WITH INTRODUCTION BY
Julia Mitchell Corbett

ABINGDON PRESS
NASHVILLE

THROUGH A GLASS DARKLY: READINGS ON THE CONCEPT OF GOD

This book is printed on acid-free paper.

Through a glass darkly.
  Includes bibliographies and index.
  1. God. I. Corbett, Julia Mitchell.
  BT102.T53   1989   211   88-8171

  ISBN 0-687-41894-1 (pbk. : alk. paper)

ISBN 0-687-41894-1

MANUFACTURED BY THE PARTHENON PRESS AT
NASHVILLE, TENNESSEE, UNITED STATES OF AMERICA

To My Daughter
Hinda Diane Mitchell

CONTENTS

PART TWO: Theological Answers

PREFACE

T HROUGH A GLASS DARKLY IS AN EDITED COLLECTION
of readings on the theme of the origin of human beings' concepts of
God. The answer to the question, "How do human concepts about
God originate?" is not self-evident, thus leading to further exploration. There
are actually two distinguishable questions here: (1) If we assume that God
does in fact exist, then how is God involved in the formation of people's
God-concepts? (2) Assume, on the other hand, that God does not exist, or that
God's existence at least cannot be proven. What, then, accounts for the
persistence of God-concepts? Further, what is the meaning of the vast
diversity of these concepts? This question is pertinent as a corollary to either
(1) or (2), above. Many people live and have lived by their belief in God, and
a not insignificant number have been willing to die for their convictions. The
sources of such a powerful concept deserve investigation.

In what follows, the two basic questions cited above form two major
categories. Scholars who do not begin with God's existence as a self-evident
fact are left with the necessity of accounting for why people have ideas about
God. Some, such as Emile Durkheim, claim that the reality behind the idea of
God is the culture or society. Others, like Feuerbach and Freud, developed
theories based on the belief that the idea of God is an illusion cast up by the
human mind. Carl Jung developed an answer that roots God images in the
larger psychic totality of the human race. Heidegger explores the function of
God images in the time of the "absence" of God. Finally, Mircea Eliade
investigates the vast diversity of images of God, and the relation between the
sacred and the profane in those images.

The distinctively theological answers begin with the affirmation of

God's existence, as found in the Christian religion; a very different set of answers (as well as different ways of posing the questions) would result if the religions of the East were included. Karl Barth represents the theological viewpoint that focuses on God's self-revelation through the Word of God in the Bible, and the Word as Jesus Christ to whom the Bible points, according to faith. Anselm, Aquinas, and Paley, while assuming that God indeed exists, offer rational explanations of why this is so, without relying on the Bible. Kant finds his answer in the demands of the moral life rather than in the life of the mind. Paul Tillich seeks to move beyond the dichotomy of "special" versus "general" revelation (or "faith" versus "reason") and to show how the experience of the whole person leads to the "God beyond the God of theism." Finally, Julian Huxley develops a wholly naturalistic approach that does away entirely with reliance on revelation.

It should be noted at the outset that the method of presentation used in this collection is phenomenological, in the broad sense of the term. That is, the readings are permitted to stand on their own, without evaluation. The editorial introductions set the authors and their works in their socio-cultural contexts and intellectual settings, without making a judgment about their veracity or value. Evaluation in matters such as these rests with the reader.

PART ONE

THE
ACADEMIC
STUDY
OF RELIGION

INTRODUCTION

THE SOCIAL-SCIENTIFIC OR ACADEMIC-HUMANISTIC approach to the investigation and interpretation of human religious life differs from the theological or devotional approach in a key cluster of ideas and commitments. Representatives of this point of view do *not* assume that God exists and is in some way involved in people's formation of ideas about God. While as individuals academicians who study religion may be theistic, atheistic, or agnostic, as scholars of religion they look in another direction, so to speak, away from God and toward the human dimension of religion. They seek as scholars to *understand*, without involving themselves in *believing*. The academic study of religion thus separates understanding and believing, in a way that Anselm, for example, who prayed for belief in order that he might understand, did not. By means of empathetic understanding, scholars can appreciate the beliefs of others as meaningful and valid for those who hold them. This is possible apart from personal commitment to that belief, without living one's own life by those commitments.

There is another way of expressing the difference between the theological or devotional and the academic study of religion. Religion is a multifaceted phenomenon. On the one hand, it looks toward an ultimate dimension, expressed in the Christian tradition by such symbols as God, heaven and hell, salvation and sin, and resurrection. On the other hand, however, religions as they develop take on a vast variety of features invented by human beings, such as beliefs, lifestyles, worship, and institutional organizations. It is these latter aspects, in their precisely human reality, that are grist for the mill of the academic study of religion.

Theologians usually understand revelation as a process involving both God's self-revelation and the human response to revelation. While revelation, presupposing as it does a revealer, is specifically a theological category, it is also possible (and valid) to concentrate one's scholarly attention on the human response to that revelation. In doing so, the academic scholar of religion seeks to understand the various human dimensions of the entire religious process.

Because of the multifaceted nature of human religiousness, several distinct academic disciplines have made religion an object for study. The various social sciences came into their own in the 1800s. The academic approach to religion, initially based primarily on the newly developing social sciences, began in Europe. The tools of reason and analysis were being used to investigate all areas of human behavior, and religion was no exception. By the latter half of the 1800s, the study of religion had taken its place alongside the other human sciences.[1]

Initially, investigators of religion attempted to delve back into history and search out the earliest origins of religion, believing that if we could determine how the earliest religions began, we would have the most important key to understanding all religion. The nature of religion was believed to be determined by its origins.

The search for origins produced several truly great scholars and theories. This must be said, even though their work was later supplanted. They were the true pioneers of the discipline. F. Max Mueller claimed in *Essays in Comparative Mythology* (1856) that the origin of religion lay in incorrect thinking on the part of less-developed "primitive" peoples. Natural objects and events such as fire, rain, wind, mountains, or the waxing and waning of the moon lead to responses such as awe, wonder, terror, or trust. The object of such emotions was then personified and regarded as an acting subject. Over time, the name became separated from the event, and a deity was born. Edward B. Tylor (*Religion in Primitive Culture*, 1871) also based his theory on the premise that "primitive" peoples' mentality was less developed than, although not inferior to, that of later peoples. The obvious differences between the living and the dead, plus the phenomenon of the appearance of humans in dreams and visions, led these people to the belief that every living being has both a visible physical aspect and an invisible soul. Thus, religion was held to originate with animism. Robert H. Codrington and Robert R. Marett both advocated theories linking the origin of religion with the experience of awe in the face of natural phenomena. Lucien Levy-Bruhl's approach was similar in that he linked religion to sensitivity to the felt presence of invisible powers.

The search for the earliest origins of religion among the "primitives" was based upon a number of assumptions, all of which were later discredited. Among these assumptions were the following: (1) All religion can be traced back to a single source; (2) religion has progressed historically from simple to complex, with the current stage being the most developed; (3) the religions of contemporary pre-literate societies reveal how religion began in archaic cultures; (4) the more technological and literate a culture is, the more advanced its religion will be.[2]

With the realization that these assumptions would not bear the weight of the theories built upon them, scholars turned to explanations of religion that focused on its psychological and social functions. These are the *functionalist* theories. They avoid the problems involved in looking back at religion's earliest origins by asking, "What role does religion play; what does it *do* now?" Religion is seen as one of several elements in the life of an individual or a culture.

Psychologists study the roles religion plays in the life of the individual. William James, regarded by many as the founder of American psychology, investigated both the effect of religious factors on personality growth and the effect of personality on religious behavior in his well-known book, *The Varieties of Religious Experience* (1902). Psychological anthropologist Clyde Kluckhohn and historian Edwin E. James cited religion's role in helping people cope with the trials and dangers of daily life and the reality of death. Humanistic psychologists such as Gordon Allport (*The Individual and His Religion*, 1950) and Rollo May (*Man's Search for Himself*, 1953) relate religion to the development of human beings' fullest potential, including the capacity for the formation of meaningful relationships with self, others, and the transcendent, however the latter is defined. Also included among psychologists who have examined religion are Sigmund Freud, the father of the psychoanalytic movement, and Carl Jung, founder of analytic psychology. For further discussion of Freud and his contribution to the discussion, see chapter 3; for fuller discussion of Jung's work, see chapter 4.

Sociologists have emphasized the roles religion plays in society or culture, rather than in the life of the individual. Clearly, however, since cultures are composed of individuals and individuals are influenced by the cultures in which they live, these two cannot, finally, be separated. Religion helps integrate individuals into a culture by providing a sense of belonging and self-definition. It helps provide order in a society by being a locus for moral values. And it gives ways by which a society can relate itself to goals and values of a transcendent nature. Emile Durkheim and Max Weber are two well-known classical sociologists of religion. Durkheim's work will be discussed in chapter 1. Weber investigated the interrelationship between religion and other social forces in specific historical periods; *The Sociology of Religion* (1922) is still a standard work. Probably his best-known work, however, is his investigation of the interaction of religion and the economic system in *The Protestant Ethic and the Spirit of Capitalism* (1930). Other contemporary sociologists noted especially for their studies of religion as a meaning system in American culture are Robert Bellah, W. Lloyd Warner, and Thomas Luckmann.

Cultural anthropologists also have taken religion seriously as a means of (1) establishing patterns of cultural self-awareness through habits such as ritual and ceremony, and (2) stabilizing a society in times of transition, such as the death of a leader and the succession of a new one. One of the best known of the cultural anthropologists is the French structuralist Claude Levi-Strauss, whose research on how myths operate to inform the deepest levels of human consciousness is contained in his three-volume *Introduction to a Science of Mythology* (1969), and *The Savage Mind* (1966). Religion, as a symbol system that operates at a pre-rational as well as a rational level, is thus a key way that life is interpreted as meaningful by both individuals and cultures.

A third avenue of approach to the academic study of religion has been and continues to be the comparative method. Beginning later than either the search for origins or the social-scientific functionalist approach, it continues to be a significant part of religious studies today. There are three subcategories in the comparative study of religion. All are united in their attempt to understand religion in various cultures and times, to investigate just what it is that is "religious" about religion, and to be descriptive rather than normative (value-setting). There is some overlap between categories.

The first subcategory, the history of religions, has two major objectives: the fullest and most objective possible description of a particular historical setting, and the description of the way religious life changes in interaction with other cultural conditions and events.[3] The focus is strictly on empirical evidence. Two well-known historians of religion, both associated with the University of Chicago (a center for history of religions scholarship), are Mircea Eliade, whose work is reviewed in chapter 6, and Joseph M. Kitagawa.

The phenomenology of religion forms the second way of approaching the history of religions. Phenomenologists investigate the question of what is religious in religious phenomena by making explicit the intention behind religious actions and beliefs. What, in other words, is the aim or reason *why* a religious person does what he or she does? A second key goal of the phenomenological method is the discovery and explication of recurrent typical patterns of religious belief and behavior. Four assumptions guide the work of phenomenologists: (1) The deepest meaning of religious phenomena is to be found in their intentional structure; (2) this meaning can best be elucidated by comparing typical patterns of religion; (3) religion has its own unique character and cannot be reduced to anything else; (4) the scholar must set aside his or her own point of view to enter empathetically into the world of the religion under investigation.[4] Rudolf Otto highlighted the unique quality of religious events as evoking both awe and fascination in The Idea of the Holy (1917). Gerardus van der Leeuw, the Dutch phenomenologist, studied religion as a unique interaction between a subject and an object in Religion in Essence and Manifestation (1933). Eliade's Patterns in Comparative Religion (1949) is a classic explication of a series of significant recurrent patterns of religious belief and action, from a phenomenological perspective.

Finally, there is a group of comparativists who attempt to give equal weight to both the uniqueness of religion and the extent to which it is influenced by its specific socio-cultural context. Joachim Wach (The Comparative Study of Religion, 1958) explicated religion in terms of its uniqueness as an intense, imperative response of a whole person to what is perceived as ultimate, which simultaneously uses modes of expression found in other than religious contexts. For example, religious perceptions evoke ritual, but so do patriotism, civil ceremonies, and the like. Wilfred Cantwell Smith has focused his studies on the element of individual human faith as a way of understanding what is religious in religion and as a means of opening up interfaith dialogue. His books include The Meaning and End of Religion (1963), Religious Diversity (1976), and Towards a World Theology: Faith and the Comparative History of Religion (1981).

Ninian Smart, a British scholar best known as a philosopher of religion, has challenged the assumption that there is a common inner core of religious experience that underlies the vast differences among religions. In The Phenomenon of Religion (1973) and The Religious Experience of Mankind (third edition, 1984), he emphasizes that a careful account of the differences is a vital part of phenomenological analysis.

Many of the academic disciplines included in the social sciences and humanities have trained the searchlight of their investigations on religion as one sphere of human activity. Investigators who are also believers and those who are not have explored and continue to explore common territory. The "academic" side of the belief versus disbelief

15

distinction is the difference of opinion between those scholars who see religion as having positive effects on the individual and the society, and those who view the effects negatively. The functionalists claim that the role of religion in the overall human economy is positive, working toward the integration of human personality and the attainment of the highest goals of which humankind is capable, aiding individuals in coping with the limit situations of life, such as birth and death, helping to ensure social cohesion, and stabilizing societies in times of crisis and transition. The dysfunctionalists, on the other hand, think that religion does more harm than good. Religion's promises of future rewards, it is held, distract people from coming to grips with the here and now. Religion alienates people from the best in themselves by ascribing all goodness and power to a deity outside humanity. It provides a false sense of both security and threat, and keeps people in a state of childlike dependence by the belief in an omnipotent parental deity. Among the authors of the reading excerpts that follow, Feuerbach and Freud are clearly dysfunctionalists, while Durkheim, Jung, Eliade, and Heidegger, along with the theologians in part 2, view religion's role positively.

It is important to recognize that there is no single correct method, no approach that can be rejected out of hand as "wrong." The choice of a method of investigation will depend, of course, on the preference and training of the scholar and on the specific questions he or she wishes to answer. In the readings that follow, philosophers, psychologists, and a sociologist are represented.

For Further Reading

Allport, Gordon W. *The Individual and His Religion*. New York: Macmillan, 1950.

Bettis, Joseph Dabney. *Phenomenology of Religion: Eight Modern Descriptions of the Essence of Religion*. New York: Harper & Row, 1969.

Capps, Walter H. *Ways of Understanding Religion*. New York: Macmillan, 1972.

Eliade, Mircea. *The Quest: History and Meaning in Religion*. Chicago: University of Chicago Press, 1969.

Eliade, Mircea, and Joseph Kitagawa, eds. *History of Religions: Essays in Methodology*. Chicago: University of Chicago Press, 1959.

Evans-Prichard, E. E. *Theories of Primitive Religion*. London: Oxford University Press, 1965.

Frazer, James G. *The New Golden Bough*. Abridged. Ed. T. H. Gaster. New York: Macmillan, 1959.

Jordan, Louis Henry. *Comparative Religion*. Atlanta: Scholars Press, 1986.

Kitagawa, Joseph. *The History of Religions: Essays on the Problem of Understanding*. Chicago: University of Chicago Press, 1967.

Lessa, W. A., and E. Z. Vogt. *Reader in Comparative Religion: An Anthropological Approach*. 3rd ed. New York: Harper & Row, 1962.

Newman, W. M., ed. *The Social Meanings of Religion: An Integrated Anthology*. Chicago: Rand McNally Publishers, 1974.

Rudolph, Kurt. *Historical Fundamentals and the Study of Religion.* New York: Macmillan, 1985.

Sharpe, Eric J. *Comparative Religion: A History.* 2nd ed. LaSalle, Ill.: Open Court Publishing Co., 1986.

Streng, Frederick J. *Understanding Religious Life.* 3rd ed. Belmont, Calif.: Wadsworth Publishing Co., 1985.

Tylor, E. B. *Religion in Primitive Culture.* New York: Harper & Row, 1958.

Weber, Max. *The Sociology of Religion.* Trans. Ephriam Fischoff. Boston: Beacon Press, 1922.

Wilson, Bryan. *Religion in Sociological Perspective.* New York: Oxford University Press, 1982.

I

SOCIETY AND THE IDEA OF GOD

1   Emile Durkheim

(1858–1917)

E MILE DURKHEIM IS ONE OF THE BEST-KNOWN CLASSICAL sociologists of religion and truly a pioneer in the development of a scientific sociology. He tried to make sociology empirical by supporting his conclusions with statistical and ethnological data.

Born in Epinal, France, of Jewish background, Durkheim decided early not to follow the tradition of his family, which favored his becoming a rabbi. Instead, he studied philosophy and upon graduating in 1882 from the Ecole Normale Supérieure chose to pursue a career in the yet-young discipline of sociology. Various professorships followed. One of Durkheim's key contributions was his founding in 1898 of *L'Année Sociologique*, a social sciences journal dedicated to the emerging scientific study of human society.

Societies, Durkheim said, have their own systems of representations, symbols, and ideas, which he named "collective representations." Collective representations are universal rather than individual, existing outside the consciousness of the individual and exercising a coercive power over it. This system is revealed to the investigator by direct examination of such cultural institutions as art, law, literature, and religion.

What a society designates by the term "God" is such a collective representation. It symbolizes the group's self-definition in terms of its highest values, projected and given divine sanction. A primary need of any social group is solidarity among its members. Social institutions— among which religion is paramount—contribute to that identity. Religion enforces the most central values of the group by such means as giving a divine or supernatural account of the group's beginnings, citing

20

a special divinely ordained role that gives meaning to the group's existence, and providing a system of divinely ordered rewards and punishments that encourage individual conformity with the aims and values of the group. Durkheim also believed that the way to individual fulfillment lies along the path of internalization of society's values and norms. Through its stories, teachings, and ritual, religion facilitates this internalization. Thus, religion makes a positive contribution to the life of both individuals and the society of which they are a part.

The crucial question for Durkheim was how a society held together: What went into the "glue" that made it all stick? Why did people accept and obey society's rules and come to make their culture's values their own? Especially in times of significant social change, understanding the factors that stabilize society is essential.

Durkheim studied the primal, totemic religion of the Australian Arunta and came to believe that one could generalize from the features of primal religion to characterize any religion per se, no matter how developed.

In his study of the Arunta's totemic beliefs, practices, and institutions, Durkheim noted that in the totemic system, three interrelated things are *all* regarded as sacred: the totemic emblem itself, the animal or plant the emblem represents, and the clan identified with that particular totemic emblem. Durkheim found a clue to the meaning of religion in this shared sacrality: The religious character has to come from something common to all three.

It is clear that the totem is above all else a symbol. Durkheim concluded that it symbolizes two things simultaneously. It gives outward, physical form to the totemic principle or the god of the clan or tribe. But it also symbolizes the clan or tribe itself, the society called into being by its relationship to this particular totem. From this analysis, Durkheim draws his conclusion: It then follows that the god and the society are themselves one, since they are both symbolized by the same thing. The totem/god is the clan or tribe itself, personified and given visible form.[1]

The totemic emblem, symbolizing as it does both the sacred and the society, means, finally, that sacred and society are one and the same thing. The relation between the individual and the sacred is precisely the individual's relation with the society, divinized and projected outward upon the cosmos. This principle, starkly simple in primal religions such as Arunta totemism, is the basis of developed religions as well.[2] God images are society writ large.

*   *   *

THE GOD OF CULTURE

. . . [Religion] is something eminently social. Religious representations are collective representations which express collective realities; the rites are a manner of acting which take rise in the midst of the assembled groups and which are destined to excite, maintain or recreate certain mental states in these groups. So if the categories are of religious origin, they ought to participate in this nature common to all religious facts; they too should be social affairs and the product of collective thought. At least—for in the actual condition of our knowledge of these matters, one should be careful to avoid all radical and exclusive statements—it is allowable to suppose that they are rich in social elements. . . .

. . . Collective representations are the result of an immense co-operation, which stretches out not only into space but into time as well; to make them, a multitude of minds have associated, united and combined their ideas and sentiments; for them, long generations have accumulated their experience and their knowledge. A special intellectual activity is therefore concentrated in them which is infinitely richer and complexer than that of the individual. From that one can understand how the reason has been able to go beyond the limits of empirical knowledge. It does not owe this to any vague mysterious virtue but simply to the fact that according to the well-known formula, man is double. There are two beings in him: an individual being which has its foundation in the organism and the circle of whose activities is therefore strictly limited, and a social being which represents the highest reality in the intellectual and moral order that we can know by observation—I mean society. This duality of our nature has as its consequence in the practical order, the irreducibility of a moral ideal to a utilitarian motive, and in the order of thought, the irreducibility of reason to individual experience. In so far as he belongs to society, the individual transcends himself, both when he thinks and when he acts. . . .

At the beginning of this work we announced that the religion whose study we were taking up contained within it the most characteristic elements of the religious life. The exactness of this proposition may now be verified. Howsoever simple the system which we have studied may

---

Reprinted by permission of The Free Press, a Division of Macmillan, Inc., and of Allen & Unwin, from Emile Durkheim, *The Elementary Forms of the Religious Life*, trans. Joseph Ward Swain (New York: The Free Press, 1965), pp. 22, 29, 462-75.

be, we have found within it all the great ideas and the principal ritual attitudes which are at the basis of even the most advanced religions: the division of things into sacred and profane, the notions of the soul, of spirits, of mythical personalities, and of a national and even international divinity, a negative cult with ascetic practices which are its exaggerated form, rites of oblation and communion, imitative rites, commemorative rites and expiatory rites; nothing essential is lacking. We are thus in a position to hope that the results at which we have arrived are not peculiar to totemism alone, but can aid us in an understanding of what religion in general is.

. . . If among certain peoples the ideas of sacredness, the soul and God are to be explained sociologically, it should be presumed scientifically that, in principle, the same explanation is valid for all the peoples among whom these same ideas are found with the same essential characteristics. . . .

Our entire study rests upon this postulate that the unanimous sentiment of the believers of all times cannot be purely illusory. . . . [T]hese religious beliefs rest upon a specific experience whose demonstrative value is, in one sense, not one bit inferior to that of scientific experiments, though different from them. We, too, think that "a tree is known by its fruits," and that fertility is the best proof of what the roots are worth. But from the fact that a "religious experience," if we choose to call it this, does exist and that it has a certain foundation—and, by the way, is there any experience which has none?—it does not follow that the reality which is its foundation conforms objectively to the idea which believers have of it. The very fact that the fashion in which it has been conceived has varied infinitely in different times is enough to prove that none of these conceptions express it adequately. . . . In order to discover what this object consists of, we must submit them to an examination and elaboration analogous to that which has substituted for the sensuous idea of the world another which is scientific and conceptual.

This is precisely what we have tried to do, and we have seen that this reality, which mythologies have represented under so many different forms, but which is the universal and eternal objective cause of these sensations *sui generis* out of which religious experience is made, is society. . . .

. . . In summing up, then, it may be said that nearly all the great social institutions have been born in religion. Now in order that these principal aspects of the collective life may have commenced by being only varied aspects of the religious life, it is obviously necessary that the religious life be the eminent form and, as it were, the concentrated expression of the whole collective life. If religion has given birth to all that is essential in society, it is because the idea of society is the soul of religion.

Religious forces are therefore human forces, moral forces. . . .

But, it is said, what society is it that has thus made the basis of religion? Is it the real society, such as it is and acts before our very eyes, with the legal and moral organization which it has laboriously fashioned during the course of history? This is full of defects and imperfections. . . .

But, on the other hand, does someone think of a perfect society, where justice and truth would be sovereign, and from which evil in all its forms would be banished for ever? No one would deny that this is in close relations with the religion sentiment; for, they would say, it is towards the realization of this that all religions strive. But that society is not an empirical fact, definite and observable; it is a fancy, a dream with which men have lightened their sufferings, but in which they have never really lived. It is merely an idea which comes to express our more or less obscure aspirations towards the good, the beautiful and the ideal. Now these aspirations have their roots in us; they come from the very depths of our being; then there is nothing outside of us which can account for them. Moreover, they are already religious in themselves; thus it would seem that the ideal society presupposes religion, far from being able to explain it. . . .

. . . Men alone have the faculty of conceiving the ideal, of adding something to the real. Now where does this singular privilege come from? Before making it an initial fact or a mysterious virtue which escapes science, we must be sure that it does not depend upon empirically determinable conditions.

The explanation of religion which we have proposed has precisely this advantage, that it gives an answer to this question. For our definition of the sacred is that it is something added to and above the real: now the ideal answers to this same definition; we cannot explain one without explaining the other. In fact, we have seen that if collective life awakens religious thought on reaching a certain degree of intensity, it is because it brings about a state of effervescence which changes the conditions of psychic activity. Vital energies are over-excited, passions more active, sensations stronger; there are even some which are produced only at this moment. A man does not recognize himself; he feels himself transformed and consequently he transforms the environment which surrounds him. In order to account for the very particular impressions which he receives, he attributes to the things with which he is in most direct contact properties which they have not, exceptional powers and virtues which the objects of every-day experience do not possess. In a word, above the real world where his profane life passes he has placed another which, in one sense, does not exist except in thought, but to which he attributes a higher sort of dignity than to the first. Thus, from a double point of view it is an ideal world.

. . . The ideal society is not outside of the real society; it is a part of it. Far from being divided between them as between two poles which mutually repel each other, we cannot hold to one without holding to the other. For a society is not made up merely of the mass of individuals who compose it, the ground which they occupy, the things which they use and the movements which they perform, but above all is the idea which it forms of itself. . . .

Thus the collective ideal which religion expresses is far from being due to a vague innate power of the individual, but it is rather at the school of collective life that the individual has learned to idealize. It is in assimilating the ideals elaborated by society that he has become capable of conceiving the ideal. It is society which, by leading him within its sphere of action, has made him acquire the need of raising himself above the world of experience and has at the same time furnished him with the means of conceiving another. For society has constructed this new world in constructing itself, since it is society which this expresses. Thus both with the individual and in the group, the faculty of idealizing has nothing mysterious about it. It is not a sort of luxury which a man could get along without, but a condition of his very existence. He could not be a social being, that is to say, he could not be a man, if he had not acquired it. It is true that in incarnating themselves in individuals, collective ideals tend to individualize themselves. Each understands them after his own fashion and marks them with his own stamp; he suppresses certain elements and adds others. Thus the personal ideal disengages itself from the social ideal in proportion as the individual personality develops itself and becomes an autonomous source of action. But if we wish to understand this aptitude, so singular in appearance, of living outside of reality, it is enough to connect it with the social conditions upon which it depends.

. . . In showing that religion is something essentially social, we do not mean to say that it confines itself to translating into another language the material forms of society and its immediate vital necessities. It is true that we take it as evident that social life depends upon its material foundation and bears its mark, just as the mental life of an individual depends upon his nervous system and in fact his whole organism. But collective consciousness is something more than a mere epipheno-menon of its morphological basis, just as individual consciousness is something more than a simple efflorescence of the nervous system. In order that the former may appear, a synthesis *sui generis* of particular consciousness is required. Now this synthesis has the effect of disengaging a whole world of sentiments, ideas and images which, once born, obey laws all their own. They attract each other, repel each other, unite, divide themselves, and multiply, though these combinations are not commanded and necessitated by the condition of the underlying reality. The life thus brought into being even enjoys so great an independence that it sometimes indulges in manifestations with no purpose or utility of any sort, for the mere pleasure of affirming itself. . . .

We have shown how the religious force which animates the clan particularizes itself, by incarnating itself in particular consciousnesses. Thus secondary sacred beings are formed; each individual has his own, made in his own image, associated to his own intimate life, bound up with his own destiny; it is the soul, the individual totem, the protecting ancestor, etc. These beings are the object of rites which the individual can celebrate by himself, outside of any group; this is the first form of the individual cult. To be sure, it is only a very rudimentary cult; but since the personality of the individual is still only slightly marked, and but little value is attributed to it, the cult which expresses it could hardly be expected to be very highly developed as yet. But as individuals have differentiated themselves more and more and the value of an individual has increased, the corresponding cult has taken a relatively greater place in the totality of the religious life and at the same time it is more fully closed to outside influences.

Thus the existence of individual cults implies nothing which contradicts or embarrasses the sociological interpretation of religion; for the religious forces to which it addresses itself are only the individualized forms of collective forces. Therefore, even when religion seems to be entirely within the individual conscience, it is still in society that it finds the living source from which it is nourished. . . .

Thus there is something eternal in religion which is destined to survive all the particular symbols in which religious thought has successively enveloped itself. There can be no society which does not feel the need of upholding and reaffirming at regular intervals the collective sentiments and the collective ideas which make its unity and its personality. Now this moral remaking cannot be achieved except by the means of reunions, assemblies and meetings where the individuals, being closely united to one another, reaffirm in common their common sentiments; hence come ceremonies which do not differ from regular religious ceremonies, either in their object, the results which they produce, or the processes employed to attain these results. What essential difference is there between an assembly of Christians celebrating the principal dates of the life of Christ, or of Jews remembering the exodus from Egypt or the promulgation of the decalogue, and a reunion of citizens commemorating the promulgation of a new moral or legal system or some great event in the national life?

For Further Reading

Alpert, Harry. *Emile Durkheim and His Sociology.* New York: Russell and Russell, 1961.

Durkheim, Emile. *Emile Durkheim on Religion: A Selection of Readings with Bibliographies.* Trans. W. S. F. Pickering and Jacqueline Redding. London: Routledge & Kegan Paul, 1975.

Wolff, Kurt H., ed. *Emile Durkheim, 1858–1917: A Collection of Essays, with Translations and a Bibliography.* Columbus, Oh.: Ohio State University Press, 1960.

II

THE
IMAGE
OF GOD AND
THE HUMAN MIND

2

Ludwig Feuerbach

(1804–1872)

FEUERBACH IS BEST KNOWN AS A RADICAL PHILOSOPHER and moralist. Born in Landshut, Bavaria, he was the son of noted jurist Paul Johann Anselm von Feuerbach. The elder Feuerbach was noted for his reform of early 1800s penal codes, humanizing them by abolishing torture and advocating a more even application of the law. Young Feuerbach's higher education began with the study of theology at Heidelberg and Berlin, and it appeared he would become a cleric. However, he soon came under the influence of Georg W. F. Hegel and in 1825 took up the study of philosophy, receiving his doctorate from Erlangen in 1828. He taught at Erlangen as a docent until 1836. At that time a scandal forced him into retirement in Bruckberg. He became known as the author of the anonymously published *Gedanken uber Tod und Unsterblichkeit,* which denounced Christianity as an inhumane and egotistical religion.

The die was cast. Feuerbach became known as a freethinker, an author of essays and reviews for the most controversial periodicals of his era, and a political radical as well. The ensuing works that flowed from Feuerbach's pen continued his attack on traditional religion and theology, as well as on speculative philosophy. Not only did he want to show the human significance and meaning of religion, but he explicated a theory that showed religion to have a dysfunctional role in human life.

The object human beings contemplate under the guise of "God," said Feuerbach, is nothing other than the highest and best attributes of humanity itself, projected outward onto another. Religion thus alienates humanity from itself; humanity, if it is to get on with fulfilling its highest potential, must reclaim those traits it has given over to God.

To those of us who have lived through the 1960s "death of God" movement in religion and have seen entire socio-political systems erected upon the premises of atheism and the apotheosis of humanity, and who are accustomed to critiques of religion from an atheistic point of view, Feuerbach's claim that theology is simply wrong-headed anthropology may not seem all that radical. At the time in which he wrote, however, Feuerbach's work *was* unique, and he stated his point of view sharply and with flair. What he wrote was bound to be regarded either as blasphemy in the first degree or as a herald of freedom from the oppression of religious institutions.

*   *   *

GOD IN OUR IMAGE

What we have hitherto been maintaining generally, even with regard to sensational impressions, of the relation between subject and object, applies especially to the relation between the subject and the religious object.

In the perceptions of the senses consciousness of the object is distinguishable from consciousness of self; but in religion, consciousness of the object and self-consciousness coincide. The object of the senses is out of man, the religious object is within him, and therefore as little forsakes him as his self-consciousness or his conscience; it is the intimate, the closest object. . . . The object of the senses is in itself indifferent—independent of the disposition or of the judgment; but the object of religion is a selected object; the most excellent, the first, the supreme being; it essentially presupposes a critical judgment, a discrimination between the divine and the nondivine, between that which is worthy of adoration and that which is not worthy. And here may be applied, without any limitation, the proposition: the object of any subject is nothing else than the subject's own nature taken objectively. Such as are a man's thoughts and dispositions, such is his God; so much worth as a man has, so much and no more has his God. Consciousness of God is self-consciousness, knowledge of God is self-knowledge. Buy his God thou knowest the man, and by the man his God; the two are identical. Whatever is God to a man, that is his heart and soul; and conversely, God is the manifested inward nature, the

From Ludwig Feuerbach, *The Essence of Christianity,* trans. George Eliot (New York: Harper & Bros., 1957), pp. 12-14, 17-20, 25-26, 29-31. Reprinted by permission of Routledge & Kegan Paul.

expressed self of a man,—religion the solemn unveiling of a man's hidden treasures, the revelation of his intimate thoughts, the open confession of his love-secrets.

But when religion—consciousness of God—is designated as the self-consciousness of man, this is not to be understood as affirming that the religious man is directly aware of this identity; for, on the contrary, ignorance of it is fundamental to the peculiar nature of religion. To preclude this misconception, it is better to say, religion is man's earliest and also indirect form of self-knowledge. Hence, religion everywhere precedes philosophy, as in the history of the race, so also in that of the individual. Man first of all sees his nature as if out of himself, before he finds it in himself. His own nature is in the first instance contemplated by him as that of another being. Religion is the childlike condition of humanity; but the child sees his nature—man—out of himself; in childhood a man is an object to himself, under the form of another man. Hence the historical progress of religion consists in this: that what by an earlier religion was regarded as objective, is now recognised as subjective; that is, what was formerly contemplated and worshipped as God is now perceived to be something human. What was at first religion becomes at a later period idolatry; man is seen to have adored his own nature. Man has given objectivity to himself, but has not recognised the object as his own nature: a later religion takes this forward step; every advance in religion is therefore a deeper self-knowledge. But every particular religion, while it pronounces its predecessors idolatrous, excepts itself—and necessarily so, otherwise it would no longer be religion—from the fate, the common nature of all religions: it imputes only to other religions what is the fault, if fault it be, of religion in general. Because it has a different object, a different tenor, because it has transcended the ideas of preceding religions, it erroneously supposes itself exalted above the necessary eternal laws which constitute the essence of religion—it fancies its object, its ideas, to be superhuman. But the essence of religion, thus hidden from the religious, is evident to the thinker, by whom religion is viewed objectively, which it cannot be by its votaries. And it is our task to show that the antithesis of divine and human is altogether illusory, that it is nothing else than the antithesis between the human nature in general and the human individual; that, consequently, the object and contents of the Christian religion are altogether human.

Religion, at least the Christian, is the relation of man to himself, or more correctly to his own nature (i.e., his subjective nature); but a relation to it, viewed as a nature apart from his own. The divine being is nothing else than the human being, or, rather, the human nature purified, freed from the limits of the individual man, made objective—i.e., contemplated and revered as another, a distinct being. All the attributes of the divine nature, are, therefore, attributes of the human nature. . . .

That which is to man the self-existent, the highest being, to which he can conceive nothing higher—that is to him the Divine Being. How then should he inquire concerning this being, what he is in himself? If God were an object to the bird, he would be a winged being: the bird knows nothing higher, nothing more blissful, than the winged condition. How ludicrous would it be if this bird pronounced: To me God appears as a bird, but what he is in himself I know not. To the bird the highest nature is the bird-nature; take from him the conception of this, and you take from him the conception of the highest being. How, then, could he ask whether God in himself were winged? To ask whether God is in himself what he is for me, is to ask whether God is God, is to life oneself above one's God, to rise up against him.

Whenever, therefore, this idea, that the religious predicates are only anthropomorphisms, has taken possession of a man, there has doubt, has unbelief, obtained the mastery of faith. And it is only the inconsequence of faint-heartedness and intellectual imbecility which does not proceed from this idea to the formal negation of the predicates, and from thence to the negation of the subject to which they relate. . . .

Thou believest in love as a divine attribute because thou thyself lovest; thou believest that God is a wise, benevolent being because thou knowest nothing better in thyself than benevolence and wisdom; and thou believest that God exists, that therefore he is a subject—whatever exists is a subject, whether it be defined as substance, person, essence, or otherwise—because thou thyself existest, art thyself a subject. Thou knowest no higher human good than to love, than to be good and wise; and even so thou knowest no higher happiness than to exist, to be a subject; for the consciousness of all reality, of all bliss, is for thee bound up in the consciousness of being a subject, of existing. God is an existence, a subject to thee, for the same reason that he is to thee a wise, a blessed, a personal being. The distinction between the divine predicates and the divine subject is only this, that to thee the subject, the existence, does not appear an anthropomorphism, because the conception of it is necessarily involved in thy own existence as a subject, whereas the predicates do appear anthropomorphisms, because their necessity—the necessity that God should be conscious, wise, good, &c.,—is not an immediate necessity, identical with the being of man, but is evolved by his self-consciousness, by the activity of his thought. I am a subject, I exist, whether I be wise or unwise, good or bad. . . .

Whatever man conceives to be true, he immediately conceives to be real (that is, to have an objective existence), because, originally, only the real is true to him—true in opposition to what is merely conceived, dreamed, imagined. The idea of being, of existence, is the original idea of truth; or, originally, man makes truth dependent on existence, subsequently, existence dependent on truth. Now God is the nature of man regarded as absolute truth,—the truth of man; but God, or, what is the same thing, religion, is as various as are the conditions under which man conceives this his nature, regards it as the highest being. These conditions, then, under which man conceives God, are to him the truth, and for that reason they are also the highest existence, or rather they are existence itself; for only the emphatic, the highest existence, is existence, and deserves this name. Therefore, God is an existent, real being, on the very same ground that he is a particular, definite being; for the qualities of God are nothing else than the essential qualities of man himself, and a particular man is what he is, has his existence, his reality, only in his particular conditions. . . .

The identity of the subject and predicate is clearly evidenced by the progressive development of religion, which is identical with the progressive development of human culture. . . .

Now, when it is shown that what the subject is lies entirely in the attributes of the subject; that is, that the predicate is the true subject; it is also proved that if the divine predicates are attributes of the human nature, the subject of those predicates is also of the human nature. But the divine predicates are partly general, partly personal. The general predicates are the metaphysical, but these serve only as external points of support to religion; they are not the characteristic definitions of religion. It is the personal predicates alone which constitute the essence of religion—in which the Divine Being is the object of religion. . . .

But here it is also essential to observe, and this phenomenon is an extremely remarkable one, characterising the very core of religion, that in proportion as the divine subject is in reality human, the greater is the apparent difference between God and man; that is, the more, by reflection on religion, by theology, is the identity of the divine and human denied, and the human, considered as such, is depreciated. The reason of this is, that as what is positive in the conception of the divine being can only be human, the conception of man, as an object of consciousness, can only be negative. To enrich God, man must become poor; that God may be all, man must be nothing. But he desires to be nothing in himself, because what he takes from himself is not lost to him, since it is preserved in God. Man has his being in God; why then should he have it in himself? Where is the necessity of positing the same thing twice, of having it twice? What man withdraws from himself, what he renounces in himself, he only enjoys in an incomparably higher and fuller measure in God. . . .

Man—this is the mystery of religion—projects his being into objectivity, and then again makes himself an object to this projected image of himself thus converted into a subject; he thinks of himself is an object to himself, but as the object of an object, of another being than himself. Thus here. Man is an object to God. . . . Thus, in and through God, man has in view himself alone. It is true that man places the aim of his action in God, but God has no other aim of action than the moral and eternal salvation of man: thus man has in fact no other aim than himself. The divine activity is not distinct from the human.

How could the divine activity work on me as its object, nay, work in me, if it were essentially different from me; how could it have a human aim, the aim of ameliorating and blessing man, if it were not itself human? . . .

God is the highest subjectivity of man abstracted from himself; hence man can do nothing of himself, all goodness comes from God. The more subjective God is, the more completely does man divest himself of his subjectivity, because God is, per se, his relinquished self, the possession of which he however again vindicates to himself. As the action of the arteries drives the blood into the extremities, and the action of the veins brings it back again, as life in general consists in a perpetual systole and diastole; so is it in religion. In the religious systole man propels his own nature from himself, he throws himself outward; in the religious diastole he receives the rejected nature into his heart again. God alone is the being who acts of himself,—this is the force of repulsion in religion; God is the being who acts in me, with me, through me, upon me, for me, is the principle of my salvation, of my good dispositions and actions, consequently my own good principle and nature,—this is the force of attraction in religion.

For Further Reading

Feuerbach, Ludwig Andreas. *Principles of the Philosophy of the Future.* Trans. Manfred Vogel. Indianapolis, Ill.: Bobbs-Merrill, 1966.

_____. *Lectures on the Essence of Religion.* Trans. Ralph Mannheim. New York: Harper & Row, 1967.

Kamenka, Eugene. *The Philosophy of Ludwig Feuerbach.* New York: Praeger Publishers, 1970.

Wartofsky, Marx W. *Feuerbach.* Cambridge: Cambridge University Press, 1977.

3

Sigmund Freud

(1856–1939)

S IGMUND FREUD IS WIDELY KNOWN AS THE FOUNDER OF the psychoanalytic movement in psychiatry. Although he was born in Moravia (now Czechoslovakia), Freud's middle-class Jewish family emigrated to Vienna, Austria, when he was but three years old. In 1873 the young Freud entered the University of Vienna, where he distinguished himself as a medical student, especially in his work in neurology. Although Freud's main interest was in research in neurology, he saw the need for a more practically oriented career. He therefore sought training in all the principal branches of medicine, concentrating on psychiatry with Theodor H. Meynert. He then went to Paris to study with Jean-Martin Charcot. Charcot's interest in the study of hysteria led Freud to study it also. In the spring of 1886, Freud began his private practice and soon was one of the leading neurologists in Europe.

Freud was known as a charming and highly cultured individual. He was a classical scholar, well read in the literature of several nations besides that of his native land. He had a profound knowledge of Greek mythology and references to it punctuate his writing. He preferred poetry and sculpture among the arts, but seems to have had very little feeling for music. His marriage in 1876 produced a long and eminently satisfying union. He and his wife had three sons and three daughters; one of the daughters, Anna, became a well-known psychoanalyst in her own right. He was unusually fond of children and thoroughly enjoyed their company. His pleasant home life and the devotion of his family would help Freud endure the vast abuse he suffered at the hands of skeptical colleagues and the public at large as his work became better known. He was known for his finely honed sense of humor, which ran to the penetrating and sardonic when criticism was leveled at him.

Freud's theories grew out of his medical practice and had their most immediate application to psychoanalysis. However, he was aware, apparently from the outset, that these theories had a broader usefulness. Psychoanalytic theory was held to be a theory of "normal" as well as "abnormal" behavior. It is in this vein that Freud turned to an analysis of religion in terms of the individual psyche.

According to Freud, religion is the product of illusory wish fulfillment. People subconsciously wish that they could remain under the protection of the powerful father of childhood, but this cannot be. So religion posits an omnipotent Father in heaven who serves the same functions for the adult as the earthly father does for the child—protection joined with the passing of judgment. Freud taught that " the gods" have three essential tasks: They help humankind cope with the fear of the natural world and with the cruelty of death, and they must compensate for the deprivations imposed by civilization.[1]

Religion's illusory fulfillment is especially damaging, Freud thought, because in it humanity confuses reality as it is with how it is wished to be. This, then, keeps people in a state of childlike dependence and prevents scientifically motivated action in the real world. It prevents "facing up to" life as it is and learning to live in light of the realities of terror, death, and deprivation.

* * *

TO FULFILL OUR DEAREST WISH

For the individual, too, life is hard to bear, just as it is for mankind in general. The civilization in which he participates imposes some amount of privation on him, and other men bring him a measure of suffering, either in spite of the precepts of his civilization or because of its imperfections. To this are added the injuries which untamed nature—he calls it Fate—inflicts on him. . . .

. . . Man's self-regard, seriously menaced, calls for consolation; life and the universe must be robbed of their terrors; moreover his curiosity, moved, it is true, by the strongest practical interest, demands an answer. . . .

For this situation is nothing new. It has an infantile prototype, of which it is in fact only the continuation. For once before one has found one-self in a similar state of helplessness: as a small child, in relation to one's parents. One had reason to fear them, and especially one's father; and yet one was sure of his protection against the dangers one knew. Thus it was natural to assimilate the two situations. Here, too, wishing played its part. . . .

In the course of time the first observations were made of regularity and conformity to law in natural phenomena, and with this the forces of nature lost their human traits. But man's helplessness remains and along with it his longing for his father, and the gods. The gods retain their threefold task: they must exorcize the terrors of nature, they must reconcile men to the cruelty of Fate, particularly as it is shown in death, and they must compensate them for the sufferings and privations which a civilized life in common has imposed on them. . . .

. . . It can clearly be seen that the possession of these ideas protects him in two directions—against the dangers of nature and Fate, and against the injuries that threaten him from human society itself. . . .Over each one of us there watches a benevolent Providence which is only seemingly stern and which will not suffer us to become a plaything of the over-mighty and pitiless forces of nature. Death itself is not extinction, is not a return to inorganic lifelessness, but the beginning of a new kind of existence which lies on the path of development to something higher. And, looking in the other direction, this view announces that the same moral laws which our civilizations have set up govern the whole universe as well, except that they are maintained by a supreme court of justice with incomparably more power and consistency. In the end all good is rewarded and all evil punished, if not actually in this form of life then in the latter existences that begin after death. In this way all the terrors, the sufferings and the hardships of life are destined to be obliterated. Life after death, which continues life on earth just as the invisible part of the spectrum joins on to the visible part, brings us all the perfection that we may perhaps have missed here. And the superior wisdom which directs this course of things, the infinite goodness that expresses itself in it, the justice that achieves its aim in it—these are the attributes of the divine beings who also created us and the world as a whole, or rather, of the one divine being into which, in our civilization, all the gods of antiquity have been condensed. The people which first succeeded in thus concentrating the divine attributes was not a little proud of the advance. It had laid open to view the father who had all along been hidden behind every divine figure as its nucleus. Fundamentally this was a return to the historical beginnings of the idea of

God. Now that God was a single person, man's relations to him could recover the intimacy and intensity of the child's relation to his father. But if one had done so much for one's father, one wanted to have a reward, or at least to be his only beloved child, his Chosen People. . . .

The religious ideas that have been summarized above have of course passed through a long process of development and have been adhered to in various phases by various civilizations. I have singled out one such phase, which roughly corresponds to the final form taken by our present-day white Christian civilization. It is easy to see that not all the parts of this picture tally equally well with one another, that not all the questions that press for an answer receive one, and that it is difficult to dismiss the contradiction of daily experience. Nevertheless, such as they are, those ideas—ideas which are religious in the widest sense—are prized as the most precious possession of civilization, as the most precious thing it has to offer its participants. . . .

In this function [of protection] the mother is soon replaced by the stronger father, who retains that position for the rest of childhood. But the child's attitude to its father is coloured by a peculiar ambivalence. The father himself constitutes a danger for the child, perhaps because of its earlier relation to its mother. Thus it fears him no less than it longs for him and admires him. The indications of this ambivalence in the attitude to the father are deeply imprinted in every religion, as was shown in *Totem and Taboo*. When the growing individual finds that he is destined to remain a child for ever, that he can never do without protection against strange superior powers, he lends those powers the features belonging to the figure of his father; he created for himself the gods whom he dreads, whom he seeks to propitiate, and whom he nevertheless entrusts with his own protection. Thus his longing for a father is a motive identical with his need for protection against the consequences of his human weakness. The defence against childish helplessness is what lends its characteristic features to the adult's reaction to the helplessness which *he* has to acknowledge—a reaction which is precisely the formation of religion. But it is not my intention to enquire any further into the development of the idea of God; what we are concerned with here is the finished body of religious ideas as it is transmitted by civilization to the individual. . . .

. . . It will be found if we turn our attention to the psychical origin of religious ideas. These, which are given out as teachings, are not precipitates of experience or end results of thinking: they are illusions, fulfillments of the oldest, strongest and most urgent wishes of mankind.

The secret of their strength lies in the strength of those wishes. . . . Thus the benevolent rule of a divine Providence allays our fear of the dangers of life; the establishment of a moral world-order ensures the fulfillment of the demands of justice, which have so often remained unfulfilled in human civilization; and the prolongation of earthly existence in a future life provides the local and temporal framework in which these wish-fulfillments shall take place. . . .

. . . What is characteristic of illusions is that they are derived from human wishes. . . . Thus we call a belief an illusion when a wish-fulfillment is a prominent factor in its motivation, and in doing so we disregard its relations to reality, just as the illusion itself sets no store by verification.

Having thus taken our bearings, let us return once more to the question of religious doctrines. We can now repeat that all of them are illusions and insusceptible of proof. . . .

[*What would people do without these illusions? Freud writes:*]

They will, it is true, find themselves in a difficult situation. They will have to admit to themselves the full extent of their helplessness and their insignificance in the machinery of the universe; they can no longer be the centre of creation, no longer the object of tender care on the part of a beneficent Providence. They will be in the same position as a child who has left the parental house where he was so warm and comfortable. But surely infantilism is destined to be surmounted. Men cannot remain children for ever; they must in the end go out into 'hostile life'. We may call this *'education to reality'*. Need I confess to you that the sole purpose of my book is to point out the necessity for this forward step?

. . . By withdrawing their expectations from the other world and concentrating all their liberated energies into their life on earth, they will probably succeed in achieving a state of things in which life will become tolerable for everyone and civilization no longer oppressive to anyone. . . .

For Further Reading

Freud, Sigmund. *Autobiography*. Trans. James Strachey. New York: W. W. Norton, 1935.
_____. *The Interpretation of Dreams*. Trans. and ed. James Strachey. New York: Basic Books, 1955.
_____. *The Origin and Development of Psychoanalysis*. Chicago: Henry Regnery Co., 1965.
_____. *Moses and Monotheism*. Trans. Katherine Jones. New York: Random House, 1967.
_____. *The Standard Edition of the Complete Psychological Works of Sigmund Freud*. 24 vols. Ed. James Strachey et al. London: Hogarth Press, 1953–64.

_____. *Totem and Taboo*. Trans. James Strachey. New York: W. W. Norton, 1950.

Fromm, Erich. *The Greatness and Limitations of Freud's Thought*. New York: Harper & Row, 1980.

Gay, Volney P. *Reading Freud: Psychology, Neurosis and Religion*. Chico, Calif.: Scholars Press, 1983.

Homans, Peter. *Theology After Freud: An Interpretive Inquiry*. Indianapolis, Ill.: Bobbs-Merrill, 1970.

Jones, Ernest. *The Life and Work of Sigmund Freud*. 3 vols. New York: Basic Books, 1953.

_____. *The Life and Work of Sigmund Freud*. Ed. and abridged by Lionel Trilling and Steven Marcus. New York: Basic Books, 1961.

III
_____

THE
OBJECTIVE
PSYCHE AND
THE IMAGE OF GOD

4   Carl G. Jung

(1875–1961)

CARL GUSTAV JUNG WAS BORN IN KESSWIL, SWITZERLAND, the son of an evangelical Lutheran pastor who influenced the rest of Jung's life, although his work took him in directions that his father could not have foretold. Jung lived in Switzerland all his life, traveling frequently, and died at Küssnacht. He studied medicine at Basel and was an assistant in psychiatry at Zurich, where the Jung Institute is today. In 1911 he became the founding president of the Analytical Psychology Society. An early collaborator and friend of Freud, and a member of the famed "Vienna Circle" that also included Alfred Adler and Otto Rank, Jung broke from his early mentor between 1912 and 1914. The disagreements between the two were professional, but the rift seems to have been deepened by personality factors.

Jung is one of the most original and creative thinkers that psychology has had among its ranks. He introduced and developed several concepts of lasting importance, many of which relate directly to his analysis of religion. The majority of these have to do with Jung's concept of the collective unconscious.

There are, according to Jung, several dimensions to the human psyche. Consciousness or rationality, centered in the ego, is just the "tip of the iceberg." Below it, to use a spatial metaphor, lies the sphere of the personal unconscious, which Freud had described. Its contents include all those experiences, ideas, and sensations that have either slipped from consciousness or have never been conscious. Here also is the storehouse of repressed wishes, fantasies, and so forth, which the conscious ego chooses not to deal with because they are unacceptable to it. This much of the psychic territory Freud had mapped. Beneath these two dimensions lies a third, and this discovery is Jung's unique contribution. He called it the Collective Unconscious or Objective Psyche. This is the psyche of the entire human race, shared by all and accumulated over time. Thus it holds the story of the evolution of the species. While the contents of the personal unconscious can in principle become conscious, the contents of the objective psyche are unconscious by nature.

Archetypes are inherited patterns of psychic functioning, patterns that through centuries of repetition have become ingrained in the human psyche. There is, says Jung, a "remarkable similarity of the human psyche at all times and in all places." Without there being any evidence of direct transmission, the same images arise across time and space. Like the physical structures of the body, the psyche has a structural dimension, which reflects similar uniformities.

These structural characteristics are formal only; in and of themselves they have no content. Jung is not reiterating the idea, long disproven, that acquired traits can be inherited. The inherited formal structure gives shape to the experiences that will be a part of the person's life. The forms act as filters or lenses that determine how experiences are to be experienced.[1]

Jung also compares the archetypes to channels. When water flows along the same path for centuries, a deep channel is carved out (e.g., the Grand Canyon). The river may dry up, but the channel remains, empty and ready to receive more water should rain fall. In like manner, psychic experience, as it occurs, flows along and is shaped by the archetypal channels that reflect centuries of human experience.[2] The network of such channels that underlies the deepest dimensions of the human psyche Jung called the collective unconscious. It is collective because it belongs to the entire human race. It is unconscious because it never becomes conscious as such. The archetypes always remain unconscious.

The archetypes do become conscious via symbols and myths. Abundant examples are to be found in the folklore of every nation, in the dreams of all people, and in the hallucinations of the mentally disturbed. It was through the comparison of these psychic products, noting similarities and parallels where there could have been no possible contact, that Jung arrived at the concept of a shared unconscious. These psychically based symbols and myths are also the root of religious images.

Most important here is the archetype that gives rise to images of the self and the processes connected with it. In the course of human evolution, consciousness broke free from the unconscious with considerable force. Like an adolescent struggling to maintain independence from the parents, the ego and the unconscious are at odds; the personality is split. The human problem is to establish a new relationship between ego and unconscious, a relationship in which neither extends its territory and control at the expense of the other. Jung calls this process "individuation," and the archetype that guides it is the self. This is also, as we shall see, the archetype from which images of God arise.

Thus, religion is profoundly functional for the human being, although it may well set individuals against their society. Without religion—not institutional, church-and-synagogue religion, but religion as participation in the dialogue between ego and self as reflected in naturally occurring numinous symbols—the individual is condemned to fragmentation. Consciousness and the unconscious go their separate and often divisive ways. Religion brings wholeness—salvation—and the beatitude that goes with it.

Jung's writing on religion is scattered widely throughout *Psychology and Religion,* from which the following reading is taken. Short selections have been grouped together under interpolated introductory comments. The numbers in parentheses are *paragraph* numbers, corresponding to the paragraph numbers in the book itself.

* * *

GOD AND GOD-IMAGE

[*To understand what Jung is saying about the origin of ideas about God, one must first look at his method, his phenomenological psychology.*]

(148) . . . To gain an understanding of religious matters, probably all that is left us today is the psychological approach. That is why I take these thought-forms that have become historically fixed, try to melt them down again and pour them into moulds of immediate experience. It is certainly a difficult undertaking to discover connecting links between dogma and immediate experience of psychological archetypes, but a

From *The Collected Works of C. G. Jung,* trans. R. F. C. Hull, Bollingen Series XX, vol. 11: *Psychology and Religion: West and East.* Copyright © 1958, 1969, by Princeton University Press. Excerpts reprinted by permission of Princeton University Press and Routledge & Kegan Paul.

study of the natural symbols of the unconscious gives us the necessary raw material.

(2) Although I have often been called a philosopher, I am an empiricist and adhere as such to the phenomenological standpoint. I trust that it does not conflict with the principles of scientific empiricism if one occasionally makes certain reflections which go beyond a mere accumulation and classification of experience. . . .

(4) . . . This standpoint is exclusively . . . concerned with occurrences, events, experiences—in a word, with facts. Its truth is a fact and not a judgment. When psychology speaks, for instance, of the motif of the virgin birth, it is only concerned with the fact that there is such an idea, but it is not concerned with the question whether such an idea is true or false in any other sense. The idea is psychologically true inasmuch as it exists. Psychological existence is subjective in so far as an idea occurs in only one individual. But it is objective in so far as that idea is shared by a society—by a *consensus gentium.*

[*Jung applies this method to a discussion of two Christian ideas pertaining to God, the Trinity, and the Christ.*]

(171) . . . Since I have no intention of involving myself in the metaphysics of the Trinity, I am free to accept the Church's own formulation of the dogma, without having to enter into all the complicated metaphysical speculations that have gathered round it in the course of history. . . . My chief object, however, is to give a detailed exposition of those psychological views which seem to me necessary if we are to understand the dogma as a symbol in the psychological sense. Yet my purpose would be radically misunderstood if it were conceived as an attempt to "psychologize" the dogma. Symbols that have an archetypal foundation can never be reduced to anything else, as must be obvious to anybody who possesses the slightest knowledge of my writings. To many people it may seem strange that a doctor with a scientific training should interest himself in the Trinity at all. But anyone who has experienced how closely and meaningfully these *représentations collectives* are bound up with the weal and woe of the human soul will readily understand that the central symbol of Christianity must have, above all else, a psychological meaning, for without this it could never have acquired any universal meaning whatever, but would have been relegated long ago to the dusty cabinet of spiritual monstrosities and shared the fate of the many-armed and many-headed gods of India and Greece. But since the dogma stands in a relationship of living reciprocity to the psyche, whence it originated in

the first place, it expresses many of the things I am endeavouring to say over again, even though with the uncomfortable feeling that there is much in my exposition that still needs improvement.

(553) . . . in what follows, I shall speak of the venerable objects of religious belief. Whoever talks of such matters inevitably runs the risk of being torn to pieces by the two parties who are in mortal conflict about those very things. This conflict is due to the strange supposition that a thing is true only if it presents itself as a *physical* fact. . . . "Physical" is not the only criterion of truth: there are also *psychic* truths which can neither be explained nor proved nor contested in any physical way. . . .

(554) Religious statements are of this type. They refer without exception to things that cannot be established as physical facts. If they did not do this, they would inevitably fall into the category of the natural sciences. . . .

(555) . . . That is why whenever we speak of religious contents we move into a world of images that point to something ineffable. We do not know how clear or unclear these images, metaphors, and concepts are in respect of their transcendental object. If, for instance, we say "God," we give expression to an image or verbal concept which has undergone many changes in the course of time. . . .

(556) If, therefore, in what follows I concern myself with these "metaphysical" objects, I am quite conscious that I am moving in a world of images and that none of my reflections touches the essence of the Unknowable. . . .

(557) I would go a step further and say that the statements made in the Holy Scriptures are also utterances of the soul—even at the risk of being suspected of psychologism. The statements of the conscious mind may easily be snares and delusions, lies, or arbitrary opinions, but this is certainly not true of the statements of the soul: to begin with they always go over our heads because they point to realities that transcend consciousness. These *entia* are the archetypes of the collective unconscious, and they precipitate complexes of ideas in the form of mythological motifs. Ideas of this kind are never invented, but enter the field of inner perception as finished products, for instance in dreams. They are spontaneous phenomena which are not subject to our will, and we are therefore justified in ascribing to them a certain autonomy. They are to be regarded not only as objects but as subjects with laws of their own. From the point of view of consciousness, we can, of course, describe them as objects, and even explain them up to a point, in the same measure as we can describe and explain a living human being. But then we have to disregard their autonomy. If that is considered, we are compelled to treat them as subjects; in other words, we have to admit

that they possess spontaneity and purposiveness, or a kind of consciousness and free will. We observe their behavior and consider their statements. This dual standpoint, which we are forced to adopt towards every relatively independent organism, naturally has a dual result. On the one hand it tells me what I do to the object, and on the other hand what it does (possibly to me). It is obvious that this unavoidable dualism will create a certain amount of confusion in the minds of my readers, particularly as in what follows we shall have to do with the archetype of Deity.

(222) . . . Religious statements are . . . never rational in the ordinary sense of the word, for they always take into consideration that other world, the world of the archetype, of which reason in the ordinary sense is unconscious, being occupied only with externals. Thus the development of the Christian idea of the Trinity unconsciously reproduced the archetype of the homoousia of Father, Son, and Ka-mutef which first appeared in Egyptian theology. . . .

(224) Thus the history of the Trinity presents itself as the gradual crystallization of an archetype that moulds the anthropomorphic conceptions of father and son, of life, and of different persons into an archetypal and numinous figure, the "Most Holy Three-in-One." . . .

(287) As a psychological symbol the Trinity denotes, first, the homoousia or essential unity of a three-part process, to be thought of as a process of unconscious maturation taking place within the individual. . . .

(288) Second, the Trinity denotes a process of conscious realization continuing over the centuries.

(289) Third, the Trinity lays claim not only to represent a personification of psychic processes in three roles, but to be the one God in three Persons, who all share the same divine nature. . . . The homoousia, whose general recognition was the cause of so many controversies, is absolutely necessary from a psychological standpoint, because, regarded as a psychological symbol, the Trinity represents the progressive transformation of one and the same substance, namely the psyche as a whole. The homoousia together with the filioque assert that Christ and the Holy Ghost are both of the same substance as the Father. But since, psychologically, Christ must be understood as a symbol of the self, and the descent of the Holy Ghost as the self's actualization in man, it follows that the self must represent something that is of the substance of the Father too. This formulation is in agreement with the psychological statement that the symbols of the self cannot be distinguished empirically from a God-image. Psychology, certainly, can do no more than establish the fact that they are indistinguishable. . . .

[*Jung reflects on the psychological meaning of the Christ symbol.*]

(229) . . . The most important of the symbolical statements about Christ are those which reveal the attributes of the hero's life: improbable origin, divine father, hazardous birth, rescue in the nick of time, precocious development, conquest of the mother and of death, miraculous deeds, a tragic, early end, symbolically significant manner of death, post-mortem effects (reappearances, signs and marvels, etc.). . . .

(230) These mythological statements, coming from within the Christian sphere as well as from outside it, adumbrate an archetype that expresses itself in essentially the same symbolism and also occurs in individual dreams or in fantasy-like projections upon living people (transference phenomena, hero-worship, etc.). The content of all such symbolic products is the idea of an overpowering, all-embracing, complete or perfect being, represented either by a man of heroic proportions, or by an animal with magical attributes, or by a magical vessel or some other "treasure hard to attain," such as a jewel, ring, crown, or, geometrically, by a mandala. This archetypal idea is a reflection of the individual's wholeness, i.e., of the self, which is present in him as an unconscious image. The conscious mind can form absolutely no conception of this totality, because it includes not only the conscious but also the unconscious psyche, which is, as such, inconceivable and irrepresentable.

(231) It was this archetype of the self in the soul of every man that responded to the Christian message, with the result that the concrete Rabbi Jesus was rapidly assimilated by the constellated archetype. In this way Christ realized the idea of the self. . . .

[*Apart from his consideration of the Christian trinitarian dogma and his psychological analysis of how the figure of the Christ came to be identified as savior, Jung addressed the question of God and God-image directly.*]

(233) The goal of psychological, as of biological, development is self-realization, or individuation. But since man knows himself only as an ego, and the self, as a totality, is indescribable and indistinguishable from a God-image, self-realization—to put it in religious or metaphysical terms—amounts to God's incarnation. That is already expressed in the fact that Christ is the son of God. And because individuation is an heroic and often tragic task, the most difficult of all, it involves suffering, a passion of the ego: the ordinary, empirical man we once were is

burdened with the fate of losing himself in a greater dimension and being robbed of his fancied freedom of will. He suffers, so to speak, from the violence done to him by the self. The analogous passion of Christ signifies God's suffering on account of the injustice of the world and the darkness of man. The human and the divine suffering set up a relationship of complementarity with compensating effects. Through the Christ-symbol, man can get to know the real meaning of his suffering: he is on the way towards realizing his wholeness. As a result of the integration of conscious and unconscious, his ego enters the "divine" realm, where it participates in "God's suffering." The cause of the suffering is in both cases the same, namely "incarnation," which on the human level appears as "individuation." The divine hero born of man is already threatened with murder; he has nowhere to lay his head, and his death is a gruesome tragedy. The self is no mere concept or logical postulate; it is a psychic reality, only part of it conscious, while for the rest it embraces the life of the unconscious and is therefore inconceivable except in the form of symbols. The drama of the archetypal life of Christ describes in symbolic images the events in the conscious life—as well as in the life that transcends consciousness—of a man who has been transformed by his higher destiny.

(757) It is only through the psyche that we can establish that God acts upon us, but we are unable to distinguish whether these actions emanate from God or from the unconscious. We cannot tell whether God and the unconscious are two different entities. Both are border-line concepts for transcendental contents. But empirically it can be established, with a sufficient degree of probability, that there is in the unconscious an archetype of wholeness which manifests itself spontaneously in dreams, etc., and a tendency, independent of the conscious will, to relate other archetypes to this centre. Consequently, it does not seem improbable that the archetype of wholeness occupies as such a central position which approximates it to the God-image. The similarity is further borne out by the peculiar fact that the archetype produces a symbolism which has always characterized and expressed the Deity. These facts make possible a certain qualification of our above thesis concerning the indistinguishableness of God and the unconscious. Strictly speaking, the God-image does not coincide with the unconscious as such, but with a special content of it, namely the archetype of the self. It is this archetype from which we can no longer distinguish the God-image empirically. We can arbitrarily postulate a difference between these two entities, but that does not help us at all. On the contrary, it only helps us to separate man from God, and prevents God from becoming man. Faith

is certainly right when it impresses on man's mind and heart how infinitely far away and inaccessible God is; but it also teaches his nearness, his immediate presence, and it is just this nearness which has to be empirically real if it is not to lose all significance. Only that which acts upon me do I recognize as real and actual. But that which has no effect upon me might as well not exist. The religious need longs for wholeness, and therefore lays hold of the images of wholeness offered by the unconscious, which, independently of the conscious mind, rise up from the depths of our psychic nature.

For Further Reading

Brown, Clifford A. *Jung's Hermeneutic of Doctrine: Its Theological Significance*. Chico, Calif.: Scholars Press, 1981.

Hanna, Charles Bartruff. *The Face of the Deep: The Religious Ideas of C. G. Jung*. Philadelphia: Westminister Press, 1967.

Jacobi, Jolande, ed. *C. G. Jung: World and Image*. Princeton, N.J.: Princeton University Press, 1979.

Jung, Carl Gustav. *Analytical Psychology: Its Theory and Practice*. New York: Random House, 1968.

_____. *Memories, Dreams, Reflections*. Recorded and ed. by Aniela Jaffé. Trans. Richard and Clara Winston. New York: Random House, 1963.

_____. *Modern Man in Search of a Soul*. Trans. W. S. Dell and Cary F. Baynes. New York: Harcourt, Brace & World, 1933.

_____. *Psychological Reflections: A New Anthology of His Writings 1905–1961*. Ed. Jolande Jacobi and R. F. C. Hull. Princeton, N.J.: Princeton University Press, 1970.

Jung, Carl Gustav, et al. *Man and His Symbols*. Garden City, N.Y.: Doubleday, 1964.

Meier, Carl Alfred. *Jung's Analytical Psychology and Religion*. Carbondale, Ill.: Southern Illinois University Press, 1977.

IV

THE PERCEPTION OF THE SACRED

5   Martin Heidegger

(1889–1976)

MARTIN HEIDEGGER WAS BORN AND RAISED ROMAN Catholic, in that area of Germany known as the Black Forest. Right from the beginning he seemed destined to pursue a career in philosophy. He received his doctorate from the University of Freiburg in 1914 and taught there until going to Marburg in 1923. In 1929 he was chosen as Husserl's successor to the Chair of Philosophy at Freiburg and in 1933, under the National Socialist regime, he was elected rector. His politics, however, led to his removal from that post a year later.

Heidegger's own philosophy, although unique, was heavily influenced by both Edmund Husserl's phenomenology and Søren Kierkegaard's existentialism. His focus is ontology, the study of Being. It is not abstract ontology that interests Heidegger, however, but Being as reflected in and by a phenomenological analysis of *Dasein*, which means human being-in-the-world. We see here his weaving together of ontological and existentialist concerns, although he steadfastly maintained that he was not an existentialist per se, a claim that is substantiated in his work. He did espouse the classical existentialist claim that "existence precedes essence" and that humans are "thrown" into existence with the freedom and responsibility to make something worthwhile out of it, a theme later picked up by Heidegger's student Jean-Paul Sartre.

Much of Heidegger's attention is directed to language, especially language as it occurs most fundamentally in poetry. Of several poets with whom Heidegger was conversant, the German Friedrich Hölderlin (1770–1843), author of odes, elegies, and hymnic works, many of which dealt with the essence of poetry itself, influenced him greatly. Language, in his view, is almost a mystical thing. It is *the* fundamental way in which human beings are human. It is the house and foundation of Being itself, as known through *Dasein,* human being-in-the-world.

The uniquely human way that humans *are* on this earth is *dwelling.* Dwelling amounts to standing within the openness of what is, the *fourfold*—earth and sky, divinities and other mortals. These four are not merely four detached things that occur together. Each is integrally a part of all the others. To dwell is to preserve what is; preserving is in its essence a letting-be as it is, an allowing to come to presence, to reveal itself. In relationship to the fourfold, this means to save the earth, receive the sky, await the divinities, and initiate other mortals. Dwelling means looking after this fourfold, taking it under our care.[1] Heidegger had no ecological program in mind when he wrote of saving the earth and receiving the sky. His was a philosophical project, a saving and receiving in an even more basic sense. This is why the poet is so important in his thought. The poet establishes this fourfold in language. In the language of the poet, earth and sky, divinities and mortals, are brought to presence, given being as they *are.*

This is one way of talking about the task of the poet. Another is to speak of the specific relation between the essential task of the poet and one element within the fourfold, the divinities or gods. Heidegger believed that his was an age of double negation, the "no more of the gods that have fled and the not-yet of the god that is coming." The gods are not a part of the present age in the way they have been in the past, ages in which the "holy names" had the power to grip people. Only as the poet names the gods again can they appear. This naming does not abolish the divine mystery; it lets it appear precisely *as* mystery. It is clear that for Heidegger there is "something" (one cannot, I think, be more specific) that is perceived by some at least as "holy." The Holy (or the gods, or the divinities) is utterly dependent upon human beings' "naming" the Holy to become available to people in any significant way. Revelation, that is to say, is a human activity. While "holy names are lacking" the gods are powerless, locked away in their own absence until the poet recalls them.

In the time of "God's failure," of God's lack, in this "time of dearth," the poet must reach deeply into the abyss. It is a dangerous time for life as a whole, but especially for the poet, who chooses to go deliberately into the abyss in the hope of retrieving a holy name and hence of naming the absent god for the people. Hölderlin's own descent into the hell of mental illness is for Heidegger a reflection of the dangers that await.

In times when the Holy is not named and hence cannot be present to humans, the "wholeness" of the whole is hidden. We cannot see things as an integrated whole—the fourfold—but as disjointed fragments only.

As the etymologies of the words themselves suggest, such a situation is not healthy. What is not "whole" is not "hale" either. There is no healing. In order to change this situation there must be mortals whose courage and passion allows them—drives them, perhaps—to confront the unholy as such, to face in their own being the danger that confronts humanity. Far more serious than any incidental peril, this is the danger inherent in cutting human nature away from Being. Hölderlin was one of those mortals who reached into this abyss and who ultimately got sucked into its bottomless vortex.[2]

Religion, for Heidegger, thus is profoundly functional. It is not the Catholicism of his youth, nor is it Christianity in any form. Most would probably call it "paganism," or perhaps humanism. It is that religiousness which transcends creed and sect and cultus, and manifests itself as a profound respect, a "letting-be" of what is truly holy: the gods, the natural world (earth and sky), and the mortals.

Religion is one of the ways, then, in which people exercise the uniquely human function of dwelling on the earth, thus constituting the world as World. Without this religiousness, "holy names are lacking" and the people perish.

* * *

NAMING THE ABSENT GOD

Why has Hölderlin's work been chosen for the purpose of showing the essence of poetry? Why not Homer or Sophocles, why not Virgil or Dante, why not Shakespeare or Goethe? The essence of poetry is realised in the works of these poets too, and more richly even, than in the creative work of Holderlin, which breaks off so early and abruptly.

This may be so. And yet Hölderlin has been chosen, and he alone. . . .

Hölderlin has not been chosen because his work, one among many, realises the universal essence of poetry, but solely because Hölderlin's poetry was borne on by the poetic vocation to write expressly of the essence of poetry. . . .

This saying forms the conclusion of the poem "Remembrance" and runs:

"But that which remains, is established by the poets." (IV. 63.)

This saying throws light on our question about the essence of poetry. Poetry is the act of establishing by the word and in the word. What is established in this manner? The permanent. But can the permanent be established then? Is it not that which has always been present? No! Even the permanent must be fixed so that it will not be carried away, the simple must be wrested from confusion, proportion must be set before what lacks proportion. That which supports and dominates the existent in its entirety must become manifest. Being must be opened out, so that the existent may appear. But this very permanent is the transitory. "Thus, swiftly passing is everything heavenly; but not in vain." (IV, 163f.) But that this should remain, is "Entrusted to the poets as a care and a service" (IV, 145). The poet names the gods and names all things in that which they are. This naming does not consist merely in something already known being supplied with a name; it is rather than when the poet speaks the essential word, the existent is by this naming nominated as what it is. So it becomes known *as* existent. Poetry is the establishing of being by means of the word. Hence that which remains is never taken from the transitory. The simple can never be picked out immediately from the intricate. Proportion does not lie in what lacks proportion. We never find the foundation in what is bottomless. Being is never an existent. But, because being and essence of things can never be calculated and derived from what is present, they must be freely created, laid down and given. Such a free act of giving is establishment.

But when the gods are named originally and the essence of things receives a name, so that things for the first time shine out, human existence is brought into a firm relation and given a basis. The speech of the poet is establishment not only in the sense of the free act of giving, but at the same time in the sense of the firm basing of human existence on its foundation.

If we conceive this essence of poetry as the establishing of being by means of the word, then we can have some inkling of the truth of that saying which Hölderlin spoke long after he had been received into the protection of the night of lunacy. . . .

We find this fifth pointer in the long and at the same time monstrous poem which begins:

"In the lovely azure there flowers with its
Metallic roof the church-tower." (VI, 24ff.)

Here Hölderlin says (line 32f.):

"Full of merit, and yet poetically, dwells
Man on this earth."

What man works at and pursues is through his own endeavours earned and deserved. "Yet"—says Hölderlin in sharp antithesis, all this does not touch the essence of his sojourn on this earth, all this does not reach the foundation of human existence. The latter is fundamentally "poetic." But we now understand poetry as the inaugural naming of the gods and of the essence of things. To "dwell poetically" means: to stand in the presence of the gods and to be involved in the proximity of the essence of things. Existence is "poetical" in its fundamental aspect— which means at the same time: in so far as it is established (founded), it is not a recompense, but a gift. . . .

. . . In a letter to a friend, immediately before leaving on his last journey to France, Hölderlin writes: "O Friend! The world lies before me brighter than it was, and more serious. I feel pleasure at how it moves onward, I feel pleasure when in summer 'the ancient holy father with calm hand shakes lightnings of benediction out of the rosy clouds.' For amongst all that I can perceive of God, this sign has become for me the chosen one. I used to be able to exult over a new truth, a better insight into that which is above us and around us, now I am frightened lest in the end it should happen with me as with Tantalus of old, who received more from the gods than he was able to digest." (V, 321.)

The poet is exposed to the divine lightnings. This is spoken of in the poem which we must recognise as the purest poetry about the essence of poetry, and which begins:

"When on festive days a countryman goes
To gaze on his field, in the morning . . ." (IV, 151ff.)

There, the last stanza says:

"Yet it behoves us, under the storms of God,
Ye poets! with uncovered head to stand,
With our own hand to grasp the very lightning-flash
Paternal, and to pass, wrapped in song,
The divine gift to the people."

And a year later, when he had returned to his mother's house, struck down with madness, Hölderlin wrote to the same friend, recalling his stay in France:

"The mighty element, the fire of heaven and the stillness of man, their life amid nature, and their limitation and contentment, have constantly seized me, and, as it is told of the heroes, I can truly say that I have been struck by Apollo." (V, 327.) The excessive brightness has driven the poet into the dark. Is any further evidence necessary as to the extreme danger of his "occupation"? The very destiny itself of the poet tells everything. The passage in Hölderlin's "Empedocles" rings like a premonition:

"He, through whom the spirit speaks, must leave betimes." (III, 154.)

And nevertheless: poetry is the "most innocent of all occupations," Hölderlin writes to this effect in his letter, not only in order to spare his mother, but because he knows that this innocent fringe belongs to the essence of poetry, just as the valley does to the mountain; for how could this most dangerous work be carried on and preserved, if the poet were not "cast out" ("Empedocles" III, 191) from the everyday life and protected *against* it by the apparent harmlessness of his occupation? . . .

The writing of poetry is the fundamental naming of the gods. But the poetic word only acquires its power of naming, when the gods themselves brings us to language. How do the gods speak?

". . . . And signs to us from antiquity are the language of the gods." (IV, 135.)

The speech of the poet is the intercepting of these signs, in order to pass them on to his own people. This intercepting is an act of receiving and yet at the same time a fresh act of giving, for "in the first signs" the poet catches sight already of the completed message and in his word boldly presents what he has glimpsed, so as to tell in advance of the not-yet-fulfilled. So:

". . . the bold spirit like an eagle
Before the tempests, flies prophesying
In the path of his advancing gods." (IV, 135.)

The establishment of being is bound to the signs of the gods. And at the same time the poetic word is only the interpretation of the "voice of the people." This is how Hölderlin names the sayings in which a people remembers that it belongs to the totality of all that exists. But often this voice grows dumb and weary. In general even it is not capable of saying of itself what is true, but has need of those who explain it. . . .

In this way the essence of poetry is joined on to the laws of the signs of the gods and of the voice of the people, laws which tend towards and away from each other. The poet himself stands between the former—the gods, and the latter—the people. He is one who has been cast out—out into that *Between*, between gods and men. But only and for the first time in this Between is it decided, who man is and where he is settling his existence. "Poetically, dwells man on this earth."

Unceasingly and ever more securely, out of the fullness of the images pressing about him and always more simply, did Hölderlin devote his poetic word to this realm of Between. And this compels us to say that he is the poet of the poet. . . .

Hölderlin writes poetry about the essence of poetry—but not in the sense of a timelessly valid concept. This essence of poetry belongs to a determined time. But not in such a way that it merely conforms to this time, as to one which is already in existence. It is that Hölderlin, in the act of establishing the essence of poetry, first determines a new time. It is the time of the gods that have fled *and* of the god that is coming. It is the time *of need*, because it lies under a double lack and a double Not: the No-more of the gods that have fled and the Not-yet of the god that is coming.

The essence of poetry, which Hölderlin establishes, is in the highest degree historical, because it anticipates a historical time; but as a historical essence it is the sole essential essence.

The time is needy and therefore its poet is extremely rich—so rich that he would often like to relax in thoughts of those that have been and in eager waiting for that which is coming and would like only to sleep in this apparent emptiness. But he holds his ground in the Nothing of this night. Whilst the poet remains thus by himself in the supreme isolation of his mission, he fashions truth, vicariously and therefore truly, for his people.

For Further Reading

Cobb, John B., Jr., and James M. Robinson, eds. *The Later Heidegger and Theology.* New York: Harper & Row, 1963.

Heidegger, Martin. *Being and Time.* Trans. John Macquarrie and Edward Robinson. New York: Harper & Row, 1962.

———. *Discourse on Thinking.* Trans. John M. Anderson and E. Hans Freund. New York: Harper & Row, 1966.

———. *On the Way to Language.* Trans. Peter D. Hertz. New York: Harper & Row, 1971.

———. *Poetry, Language, Thought.* Trans. Albert Hofstadter. New York: Harper & Row, 1971.

———. *What Is Called Thinking?* Trans. Fred D. Wieck and J. Glenn Gray. New York: Harper & Row, 1968.

Kocklemans, Joseph J. *Martin Heidegger: A First Introduction to His Philosophy.* Trans. Therese Schrynemakers. Pittsburgh: Duquesne University Press, 1965.

Macquarrie, John. *Martin Heidegger.* Richmond, Va.: John Knox Press, 1968.

Richardson, William J. *Heidegger: Through Phenomenology to Thought.* The Hague: Martinus Nijhoff, 1963.

Vycinas, Vincent. *Earth and Gods: An Introduction to the Philosophy of Martin Heidegger.* The Hague: Martinus Nijhoff, 1961.

6   Mircea Eliade

(1907–1986)

MIRCEA ELIADE WAS BORN IN ROMANIA, AND HIS student days were passed at the universities of Bucharest and Calcutta. He was emeritus professor of the history of religions at the University of Chicago, having served as chair of the history of religion there. He also taught at the University of Bucharest and at the Ecole des Hautes Etudes (Sorbonne) in Paris.

Eliade's work reflects his concern to give due emphasis both to the culturally conditioned forms that human religion takes and to the religious intention that animates these forms and gives them their religious character. Humanity perceives "the sacred" through many forms or "modalities," and different ones reflect different characteristics of the sacred.

People, according to Eliade, have a universal need to bring some sort of symbolic order to life, and it is here that religion serves human needs. Without this order, we are less than human. Religion is a crucial part of the full development of which people are capable.

Images of divinity, the holy, or the sacred—for here, "God" is far too narrow a term—grow out of human experiences of the sacred in and through ordinary, everyday reality. Things, places, events, and people of the "profane" world thus become hierophanies, manifestations of the sacred capable of revealing an ultimate order of reality and relating the rest of human life to that reality.

Eliade recognized at least four categories of hierophany:

1. Cosmic hierophanies—sky, water, earth
2. Biological hierophanies—rhythms of sun and moon, vegetation, sexuality

3. Local hierophanies—sacred places
4. Myths and symbols

In summarizing the major concerns that have animated Eliade's interpretation of religion, Wendell C. Beane and William G. Doty, in an edited collection of Eliade readings, observe that there are three directives that Eliade follows:

1. The need to recognize, on the basis of cumulative investigations by scholars from various disciplines, that sacred words and things always point beyond themselves to what Eliade calls "a meta-empirical reality and purpose" (i.e., they are material means to *spiritual* ends).

2. The need to adopt an attitude of radical displacement of one's personal biases concerning what "ought" to be thought, said, and done by other religious peoples, in order to begin not only to understand *how* religious symbols relate to their historical environment, but also *what* such symbols *intend* as sacred realities worth discovering again and again.

3. The need to compare and integrate the elements of religious traditions as a means of arriving at even tentative generalizations about humankind's religious ways of being in the world, which may lead us to understand anew the essential relation between the *human* and the *religious*.[1]

In each of the these three guidelines, which Mircea Eliade follows meticulously from the earliest beginnings of his work to the end of it, we see the open-mindedness and freedom from bias that characterize the phenomenology of religion at its best. Eliade is a most fitting author with whom to bring our survey of the formation of human images of God to a close.

* * *

THE MODALITIES OF THE SACRED

. . . [A] religious phenomenon will only be recognized as such if it is grasped at its own level, that is to say, if it is studied *as* something religious. To try to grasp the essence of such a phenomenon by means of physiology, psychology, sociology, economics, linguistics, art or any other study is false; it misses the one unique and irreducible element in

---

From Mircea Eliade, *Patterns in Comparative Religion*, trans. Rosemary Sheed (New York: Sheed & Ward, 1958), pp. xii, 1-2, 11, 13, 29, 38-40, 154-63, 216, 367-68, 445-47. Reprinted by permission of Sheed & Ward, 115 E. Armour Blvd., Kansas City, MO 64141.

it—the element of the sacred. Obviously there are no *purely* religious phenomena; no phenomenon can be solely and exclusively religious. Because religion is human it must for that very reason be something social, something linguistic, something economic—you cannot think of man apart from language and society. But it would be hopeless to try and explain religion in terms of any one of those basic functions which are really no more than another way of saying what man is. It would be as futile as thinking you could explain *Madame Bovary* by a list of social, economic and political facts; however true, they do not affect it as a work of literature.

I do not mean to deny the usefulness of approaching the religious phenomenon from various different angles; but it must be looked at first of all in itself, in that which belongs to it alone and can be explained in no other terms. . . .

1. "Sacred" and "Profane"

All the definitions given up till now of the religious phenomenon have one thing in common: each has its own way of showing that the sacred and the religious life are the opposite of the profane and the secular life. . . .

. . . If we want to limit and define the sacred, we shall have to have at our disposal a manageable number of expressions of religion. If it starts by being difficult, the diversity of those expressions becomes gradually paralysing. We are faced with rites, myths, divine forms, sacred and venerated objects, symbols, cosmologies, theologoumena, consecrated men, animals and plants, sacred places, and more. And each category has its own morphology—of a branching and luxuriant richness. We have to deal with a vast and ill-assorted mass of material. . . . Each must be considered as a hierophany in as much as it expresses in some way some modality of the sacred and some moment in its history; that is to say, some one of the many kinds of experience of the sacred man has had. Each is valuable for two things it tells us: because it is a hierophany, it reveals some modality of the sacred; because it is a historical incident, it reveals some attitude man has had towards the sacred. . . .

We must get used to the idea of recognizing hierophanies absolutely everywhere, in every area of psychological, economic, spiritual and social life. Indeed, we cannot be sure that there is *anything*—object, movement, psychological function, being or even game—that has not at some time in human history been somewhere transformed into a hierophany. It is a very different matter to find out *why* that particular thing should have become a hierophany, or should have stopped being one at any given moment. But it is quite certain that anything man has ever handled, felt, come in contact with or loved *can* become a hierophany. . . .

. . . The dialectic of a hierophany implies a more or less clear choice, a singling-out. A thing becomes sacred in so far as it embodies (that is, reveals) something other than itself. . . . for it only becomes a hierophany at the moment of stopping to be a mere profane something, at the moment of acquiring a new "dimension" of sacredness. . . .

In fact, this paradoxical coming-together of sacred and profane, being and non-being, absolute and relative, the eternal and the becoming, is what every hierophany, even the most elementary, reveals. . . . This coming-together of sacred and profane really produces a kind of breakthrough of the various levels of existence. It is implied in every hierophany whatever, for every hierophany shows, makes manifest, the coexistence of contradictory essences: sacred and profane, spirit and matter, eternal and non-eternal, and so on. . . . the sacred may be seen under any sort of form, even the most alien. . . .

11. The Sacredness of the Sky

The most popular prayer in the world is addressed to "Our Father who art in heaven". It is possible that man's earliest prayers were addressed to the same heavenly father. . . .

We shall look at a series of divine figures of the sky, but first it is necessary to grasp the religious significance of the sky as such. There is no need to look into the teachings of myth to see that the sky itself directly reveals a transcendence, a power and a holiness. Merely contemplating the vault of heaven produces a religious experience in the primitive mind. This does not necessarily imply a "nature-worship" of the sky. To the primitive, nature is never purely "natural". The phrase "contemplating the vault of heaven" really means something when it is applied to primitive man, receptive to the miracles of every day to an extent we find it hard to imagine. Such contemplation is the same as a revelation. The sky shows itself as it really is: infinite, transcendent. The vault of heaven is, more than anything else, "something quite apart" from the tiny thing that is man and his span of life. The symbolism of its transcendence derives from the simple realization of its infinite height. "Most High" becomes quite naturally an attribute of the divinity. The regions above man's reach, the starry places, are invested with the divine majesty of the transcendent, of absolute reality, of everlastingness. Such places are the dwellings of the gods; certain privileged people go there as a result of rites effecting their ascension into heaven; there, according to some religions, go the souls of the dead. The "high" is something inaccessible to man as such; it belongs by right to superhuman powers and beings; when a man ceremonially ascends the steps of a sanctuary, or the ritual ladder leading to the sky he ceases to be a man; the souls of the privileged dead leave their human state behind when they rise into heaven.

All this derives from simply contemplating the sky; but it would be a great mistake to see it as a logical, rational process. The transcendental quality of "height", or the supra-terrestrial, the infinite, is revealed to man all at once, to his intellect as to his soul as a whole. The symbolism is an immediate notion of the whole consciousness, of the man, that is, who realizes himself as a man, who recognizes his place in the universe; these primeval realizations are bound up so organically with his life that the same symbolism determines both the activity of his subconscious and the noblest expressions of his spiritual life. It really is important, therefore, this realization that though the symbolism and religious values of the sky are not deduced logically from a calm and objective observation of the heavens, neither are they exclusively the product of mythical activity and non-rational religious experience. Let me repeat: even before any religious values have been set upon the sky it reveals its transcendence. The sky "symbolizes" transcendence, power and changelessness simply by being there. It exists because it is high, infinite, immovable, powerful. . . .

When this hierophany became personified, when the divinities *of* the sky showed themselves, or took the place of the holiness of the sky as such, is difficult to say precisely. What is quite certain is that the sky divinities have always been supreme divinities; that their hierophanies, dramatized in various ways by myth, have remained for that reason sky hierophanies; and that what one may call the history of sky divinities is largely a history of notions of "force", of "creation", of "laws" and of "sovereignty." . . .

47. The Moon and Time

The sun is always the same, always itself, never in any sense "becoming". The moon, on the other hand, is a body which waxes, wanes and disappears, a body whose existence is subject to the universal law of becoming, of birth and death. The moon, like man, has a career involving tragedy, for its failing, like man's, ends in death. For three nights the starry sky is without a moon. But this "death" is followed by a rebirth: the "new moon". The moon's going out, in "death", is never final. . . .

This perpetual return to its beginnings, and this ever-recurring cycle make the moon *the* heavenly body above all others concerned with the rhythms of life. It is not surprising, then, that it governs all those spheres of nature that fall under the law of recurring cycles: waters, rain, plant life, fertility. . . . Even in the Ice Age the meaning of the moon's phases and their magic powers were clearly known. . . .

65

Time as governed and measured by the phases of the moon might be called "living" time. It is bound up with the reality of life and nature, rain and the tides, the time of sowing, the menstrual cycle. A whole series of phenomena belonging to totally different "cosmic levels" are ordered according to the rhythms of the moon or are under their influence. . . .

The moon measures, but it also unifies. Its "forces" or rhythms are what one may call the "lowest common denominator" of an endless number of phenomena and symbols. The whole universe is seen as a pattern, subject to certain laws. The world is no longer an infinite space filled with the activity of a lot of disconnected autonomous creatures: within that space itself things can be seen to correspond and fit together. All this, of course, is not the result of a reasoned analysis of reality, but of an ever clearer intuition of it in its totality. . . .

48. The Coherence of All Lunar Epiphanies

Such a whole could certainly never be grasped by any mind accustomed to proceeding analytically. And even by intuition modern man cannot get hold of all the wealth of meaning and harmony that such a cosmic *reality* (or, in fact, sacred reality) involves in the primitive mind. . . .

The "powers" of the moon are to be discovered not by means of a succession of analytical exercises, but by intuition; *it reveals itself* more and more fully. . . .

. . . If you want to express the multiplicity of lunar hierophanies in a single formula, you may say that they reveal life repeating itself rhythmically. All the values of the moon, whether cosmological, magic or religious, are explained by its modality of *being*: by the fact that it is "living", and inexhaustible in its own regeneration. . . .

. . . A sacred thing, whatever its form and substance, is sacred because it reveals or shares in ultimate *reality*. Every religious object is always an "incarnation" of something: of the *sacred*. . . .

Consequently, the moon is no more adored in *itself* than any other object, but in what it reveals of the sacred, that is, in the power centered in it, in the inexhaustible life and reality that it manifests. . . .

49. The Moon and the Waters

Both because they are subject to rhythms (rain and tides), and because they sponsor the growth of living things, waters are subject to the moon. . . .

All the moon divinities preserve more or less obvious water attributes or functions. . . .

From the earliest times it was recognized that rainfall followed the phases of the moon. . . .

Flood corresponds to the three days of darkness, or "death", of the moon. It is a cataclysm, but never a final one, for it takes place under the seal of the moon and the waters, which are pre-eminently the sign of growth and regeneration. A flood destroys simply because the "forms" are old and worn out, but it is always followed by a new humanity and a new history. . . .

50. The Moon and Vegetation

That there was a connection between the moon, rain and plant life was realized before the discovery of agriculture. The plant world comes from the same source of universal fertility, and is subject to the same recurring cycles governed by the moon's movements. . . .

. . . The metaphysical role of the moon is to *live* and yet remain *immortal*, to undergo death, but as a rest and regeneration, never as a conclusion. This is the destiny which man is trying to conquer for himself in all the rites, symbols and myths—rites, symbols and myths in which, as we have seen, the sacred values of the moon exist together with those of water and of vegetation, whether the latter derive their sacredness from the moon, or constitute autonomous hierophanies. In either case we are faced with an *ultimate reality*, a source of power and of life from which all living forms spring, either of its substance, or as a result of its blessing. . . .

74. Stones as Manifesting Power

The hardness, ruggedness, and permanence of matter was in itself a hierophany in the religious consciousness of the primitive. And nothing was more direct and autonomous in the completeness of its strength, nothing more noble or more awe-inspiring, than a majestic rock, or a boldly-standing block of granite. Above all, stone *is*. It always remains itself, and exists of itself; and, more important still, it *strikes*. Before he even takes it up to strike, man finds in it an obstacle—if not to his body, at least to his gaze—and ascertains its hardness, its roughness, its power. Rock shows him something that transcends the precariousness of his humanity: an absolute mode of being. Its strength, its motionlessness, its size and its strange outlines are none of them human; they indicate the presence of something that fascinates, terrifies, attracts and threatens, all at once. In its grandeur, its hardness, its shape and its colour, man is faced with a reality and a force that belong to some world other than the profane world of which he is himself a part.

We can hardly say that men have always adored stones simply as stones. The devotion of the primitive was in every case fastened on something beyond itself which the stone incorporated and expressed. . . .

140. Hierophanies and Repetition

Every kratophany and hierophany whatsoever transforms the place where it occurs: hitherto profane, it is thenceforward a sacred area. . . .

In fact the idea of a sacred place involves the notion of repeating the primeval hierophany which consecrated the place by marking it out, by cutting it off from the profane space around it. In the next chapter I shall show how a similar idea of repetition underlies the idea of sacred time, and is the basis of innumerable ritual systems as well as, in general, of the hopes all religious men entertain in regard to personal salvation. A sacred place is what it is because of the permanent nature of the hierophany that first consecrated it. . . . There, in that place, the hierophany repeats itself. . . .

The continuity of hierophanies is what explains the permanence of these consecrated spots. . . .

[168. Infantilization]

For the moment, let us simply note the fact of the coexistence in primitive as well as developed societies of a coherent symbolism alongside an infantilized one. We will lay aside the problem of what causes this infantilization and the question whether it may be simply the effect of the human condition as such. Here we need only realize clearly that, whether coherent or degenerate, the symbol always has an important part to play in all societies. Its function remains unchanged: it is to transform a thing or an action into *something other* than that thing or action appears to be in the eyes of profane experience. . . .

169. Symbols and Hierophanies

Seen in this way, the symbol is carrying further the dialectic of the hierophany: everything not directly consecrated by a hierophany becomes sacred because of its participation in a symbol. . . .

From these considerations it is clear that the majority of hierophanies are susceptible of becoming symbols. But the important part played by symbolism in the magico-religious experience of mankind is not due to this convertibility of hierophanies into symbols. It is not only because it continues a hierophany or takes its place that the symbol is important; it is primarily because it is able to carry on the process of hierophanization and particularly because, on occasions, it is *itself* a hierophany—it itself reveals a sacred or cosmological reality which no other manifestation is capable of revealing. . . .

Further, while a hierophany presupposes a break in religious experience (for there always exists, in one form or another, a *breach* between the sacred and the profane and a *passage* from one to the other—which breach and passage constitute the very essence of religious life), symbolism effects a permanent solidarity between man and the sacred (though this is somewhat indistinct in that man only becomes conscious of it from time to time).

For Further Reading

Eliade, Mircea. *The Myth of the Eternal Return or Cosmos and History.* Trans. Willard R. Trask. Princeton, N.J.: Princeton University Press, 1954.
———. *Myth and Reality.* Trans. Willard R. Trask. New York: Harper & Row, 1963.
———. *From Primitives to Zen: A Thematic Sourcebook of the History of Religions.* New York: Harper & Row, 1967.
———. *The Quest: History and Meaning in Religion.* Chicago: University of Chicago Press, 1969.
———. *The Sacred and the Profane: The Nature of Religion.* Trans. Willard R. Trask. New York: Harcourt Brace Jovanovich, 1959.
Altizer, Thomas. *Mircea Eliade and the Dialectic of the Sacred.* Philadelphia: Westminster Press, 1963.

PART TWO

THEOLOGICAL
ANSWERS

INTRODUCTION

T HE VARIOUS ANSWERS HERE SURVEYED HAVE IN COMMON as their beginning point the assumption that God does, in fact, exist, and is somehow involved in the formation of human ideas about God. These answers, in other words, come from within what Paul Tillich calls the "theological circle," defined by committed belief in God as the beginning point of reflection about God.[1]

The concept of revelation has been of central importance to all three major Western religions—Judaism, Christianity, and Islam—since their inceptions. This importance is entailed directly by the understanding of God in these religious traditions. God is viewed as personal and as very much involved in the ongoing life of the world and the creatures in it. God (to speak anthropomorphically) wants to communicate with human beings. This, then, gives us the basic meaning of the term "revelation": God's communication with people. This, it will be seen, further presupposes two distinct "parties" to the exchange: a God who reveals, and human beings who receive the revelation. As a communication, revelation is a two-part process, incomplete without *both* parts: speaking *and* hearing, writing *and* reading, acting *and* seeing. We will concern ourselves only with the idea of revelation in the Christian tradition.

Within that basic framework, at least four sets of interrelated questions have been important in the development of the idea. One concerns exactly what it is that is communicated or revealed in revelation. Two understandings of this have been prominent. The historically dominant view is referred to as *propositional revelation*. That which God reveals is said to be a body of knowledge about God that can be set down in propositional form. These propositions are of divine authorship and hence guaranteed to be true. Faith, then, is understood primarily in terms of obedient assent to these propositions. The Bible is seen as the book in which these truths are recorded and made available to all people.

This propositional view of revelation has frequently been superseded in more recent scholarship by an interpretation which holds that what God reveals is not propositional knowledge but God's Self, on the analogy of self-disclosure in interpersonal relationships. We may call this an *encounter* view of revelation. Its locus is not propositions but events, events in which God's character, nature, and intentions are revealed. Because these events, which for Christians center around God's actions in the history of Israel and in the life, death, and resurrection of Jesus the Christ, are believed to be salvific, this view is referred to as the *Heilsgeschichtliche* ("salvation history") view. The Bible, then, is understood as the human record of these events in which God makes God known, and faith, no longer merely intellectual assent, becomes the response of the whole person, in trust, obedience, and love, to the revelation. In other words, the proper human response to revelation is not "Yes, there is a God" but "Thou art my God."

A second distinction between general and special revelation has often been made. This distinction has been a part of Christian theological thinking since its inception. It is not too farfetched to suggest that this differentiation is found even in the Bible itself. For example, according to the author of John's Gospel, Jesus says, "I am the way, the truth, and the life," while the psalmist tells us that the entire earth and heaven show God's handiwork and glory.[2] What is at stake in this distinction is whether human beings can have knowledge of God apart from the special revelation in the history of Israel and the life of Jesus to which the Bible points.

Proponents of *general revelation* point out that their perspective avoids the thorny problem of those individuals and cultures who, through no fault of their own, have never been exposed to God's self-revelation in Jesus of Nazareth. Through general revelation, God has provided for them. It is also said that the concept of general revelation is consonant with humankind having been created in God's image, a central assertion of both Judaism and Christianity. If all of humanity is created in God's image, then all humanity is capable of at least some knowledge of God. Positing general revelation also avoids restricting God's self-disclosing activity to one sphere only.

Significant philosophical arguments attempting to demonstrate the existence of God apart from special revelation have been of three types:

A priori arguments begin with the concept or idea of God and attempt to show that the idea itself entails the existence of the being to whom it refers. Anselm's ontological argument illustrates this type. On the other hand, a variety of *a posteriori* arguments begin with some observable or demonstrable facet of human experience and seek to show that the existence of God is required to explain that facet of experience. Thomas Aquinas's five proofs of God's existence are of this type, as is William Paley's argument from the order of the world of nature. Immanuel Kant, in the third place, begins with the human experience of the moral life and a denial that God's existence can be "proven" by critical reasoning. It is, however, required as an axiom of practical reason when practical reason reflects upon the moral life.

Protestantism, especially, based on the thought of Luther and Calvin, holds that God as Creator and Sustainer of the world has left traces of God throughout creation. However, since the Fall, human ignorance and, even more, human sinfulness render people incapable of correctly perceiving those traces. This makes *special revelation* necessary. This view of revelation holds that whatever traces of God there might be in the world, God's principal revelation occurs through God's intervention in the history of the Jewish people and most significantly, for Christians, in the final revelation ("final" in the sense of *telos*, the endpoint toward which all moves) in the life, death, and resurrection of the Christ, Jesus of Nazareth. There is a strong connection with the *Heilsgeschichtliche* or salvation-historical interpretation, so named because it focuses on historical events believed to be salvific rather than on the natural world and/or human experience. Its aim is soteriological in another sense as well, in that in special revelation God is revealed specifically as the Judge and Savior of humankind.

General and special revelation need not be, and historically have not always been, seen in strident opposition to each other. Many theologians—Justin Martyr, Augustine, Aquinas, Anselm, John Calvin, John Wesley, and more recently process theologians—have used both views in ways that preserve the strengths of each and allow them to complement each other. For example, it has been said by Aquinas that knowledge of God as the Supreme Being and Creator/Sustainer of the world is available through general revelation, whereas God's trinitarian essence must be apprehended through special revelation. Special revelation may be held to be necessary to give *saving* knowledge, or as a compensation for human ignorance and sin, without denying completely the possibility of general revelation.

The distinction between general and special revelation leads directly to the third distinction often made, that between "natural" and "revealed" theology or religion. If theology is understood as systematic reflection upon the teachings of Christian faith, then the parallel is very close: *Natural theology* is reflection upon that body of teachings about God that humans can discover without supernatural divine aid, whereas *revealed theology* reflects upon the knowledge available via special revelation. Julian Huxley, for example, develops an argument that holds that people can discover *all* that is necessary without recourse to revelation. The other six theologians do not go this far, maintaining some sort of balance between the two.

The final distinction is between reason and faith and the roles they play in human knowledge of God. One extreme is represented by *fideism*, which emphasizes faith at the expense of reason. The second-century lawyer-theologian Tertullian, for example, declared "*Credo que absurdam*," "I believe because it is absurd." John Calvin also, as a result of his teaching that every human endeavor, including thought, bears the taint of sin ("total depravity"), put much more emphasis on God-given faith than on human reason, although he saw a role for each. *Deism*, at the other extreme, denied any need for revelation and faith, insisting that all necessary and valid religious truth is available through the use of reason alone.

Conservative theologian E. J. Carnell has recently advocated a point of view that gives reason a normative role alongside faith. Since people are rational creatures, spiritual commitments must not outstrip what reason finds acceptable. Faith, which is "saving faith," follows evidence. Part of why Jesus' teachings can be accepted as those of the Christ hinges on their *not* being "logical nonsense." Carnell, in other words, while not relying solely on human reason, insists that faith must not affront reason and logic, either.[3] A similarly carefully balanced account is provided by liberal Christian theologian L. Harold DeWolf.

While natural and revealed theology may legitimately be distinguished, both are utterly dependent upon God's communication to people. Such an act requires both God's revelation and human beings' active role in seeking and discovering it. God's most dramatic, arresting revelatory act remains but an attempt at revelation unless and until it is received by a rational human being. Likewise, the most intelligent person could discover nothing about God if God did not reveal it.[4]

In sum, there are four sets of distinctions here, which are best viewed as distinctions rather than iron-clad separations. If we understand revelation as a process requiring both a giver and a receiver, the parallels can be summarized as follows:

1. Emphasis on the role of the giver	1. Emphasis on the role of the receiver
2. Special revelation	2. General revelation
3. Revealed theology	3. Natural theology
4. Faith	4. Reason

What is given is, on the analogy of interpersonal relationships, both information about God (propositional revelation) and a living encounter with God. Like the other three, these two are not mutually exclusive.

For Further Reading

Baillie, John. *The Idea of Revelation in Recent Thought.* New York: Columbia University Press, 1956.

Brunner, Emil. *Revelation and Reason.* Trans. Olive Wyon. Philadelphia: Westminster Press, 1946.

Horton, Walter M. "Revelation." In *A Handbook of Christian Theology,* eds. Arthur A. Cohen and Marvin Halverson, pp. 327-28. Nashville: Abingdon Press, 1958.

Niebuhr, H. Richard. *The Meaning of Revelation.* New York: Macmillan, 1941.

I

SPECIAL
REVELATION

Karl Barth

(1886–1968)

K ARL BARTH IS QUITE POSSIBLY THE BEST-KNOWN TWEN-
tieth-century Protestant theologian, and certainly is one of the
most prolific. Upon completion of his studies, Barth, a staunch
member of the Swiss Reformed Church, held pastorates in Switzerland
until joining the theological faculty at the University of Bonn, Germany.
Summarily dismissed from this post in 1935 by the Hitler regime, he
soon returned to Basel and taught theology at the university there until
his retirement in 1962. Although his theological style was vigorously
polemical, he was described as a cheerful, fun-loving person, brisk and
with a sparkling sense of humor and an imposing countenance. Even
those nurtured in the exacting tradition of German theological studies
were awed by the depth and scope of Barth's knowledge. Yet this was a
person who was more than a theologian, who loved the music of Mozart
and often relaxed after a hard day of thinking and writing with a drink
and a smoke or a visit to a theater.[1]

It is not saying too much to say, as Heinz Zahrnt does, that the work of
Barth marks a turning point in Protestant theology. Zahrnt compares
Barth's position at the beginning of the twentieth century to that of
Schleiermacher at the dawn of the previous one. His work marks the
beginning of a new era in theology. Theology after Barth had to be done
differently if it was not to fade into intellectual oblivion. Barth
confronted the question of whether theologians could justify speaking
about God at all, given the yawning gap between God and humankind. In
that confrontation, new terms for doing theology were set forth.[2]

The answer that he gave to that question, the answer he sought to
hammer home to his readers and hearers throughout his career, was a

resounding "Yes!" Theologians have not only a right but a responsibility to speak about God, but only because God, in first addressing humankind, has given that right. Barth was trained, as were most Protestants of his time, under the influence of post-Schleiermacherian liberalism. This approach to theological thinking emphasized accommodation with culture and had an optimistic view of human goodness and possibility. In the wake of the tragedy of World War I, Barth could no longer accept these assumptions. Like Martin Luther before him, he turned to the biblical letter to the Romans. Barth discovered from his reading of Romans that talking about God in terms that accommodated God to the culture was not the way to speak meaningfully about God. In order to have anything worth saying, the theologian must begin with the realization that God comes to the culture from outside it, preserving God's otherness and independence from all that is human. God is the radically, wholly Other, and God's address to humankind is far more important than humankind's talking about God.[3]

Whereas Schleiermacher and his followers had put humanity at the center of the theological enterprise, Barth's endless preoccupation became safeguarding the sovereignty of God and the divine initiative in revelation. His sometimes intemperate attack on natural theology and on "religion" (the human attempt to reach God) in the name of "faith" (the gift of God) stems directly from his conviction that any attempt on humankind's part to discover God apart from God's self-revelation imperils God's initiative and sovereignty.

Barth's magnum opus, Dei Kirchliche Dogmatik, is translated into English as Church Dogmatics. Its title echoes his insistence that the church, the community in which revelation is received and God's Word proclaimed, is the only proper locus for doing theology. Zahrnt ascribes the greatness of Church Dogmatics to Barth's being totally caught up in what he had to say. It is Barth's single-minded focus on the power and glory of God, far removed from concerns about modernity and success, that gives the work its power. He bears witness to a triumphant God, and that note of triumph echoes in the work itself.[4]

In the reading that follows, taken from Church Dogmatics, Barth orchestrates everything he says—the knowability of God, the readiness of human beings for that knowledge, the hiddenness of God, and the truth of knowledge about God—around the theme of the absolute priority of God. It is an outstanding example of Protestantism's emphasis on special revelation as the one source of truth about God.

* * *

"THUS SAITH THE LORD"

The possibility of the knowledge of God springs from God, in that He is Himself the truth and He gives Himself to man in His Word by the Holy Spirit to be known as the truth. It springs from man, in that, in the Son of God by the Holy Spirit, he becomes an object of the divine good-pleasure and therefore participates in the truth of God.

1. The Readiness of God

To ask about the "knowability" of God is to ask about the possibility on the basis of which God is known. It is to look back from the knowledge of God and to ask about the presuppositions and conditions on the basis of which it comes about that God is known. . . .

We must begin with the fact that there is a readiness of God to be known as He actually is known in the fulfilment in which the knowledge of God is a fact. In the first instance and decisively the knowability of God is this readiness of God Himself. "God is knowable" means: "God can be known"—He can be known of and by Himself. In His essence, as it is turned to us in His activity, He is so constituted that He can be known by us.

But obviously we are not going far enough if we try to be satisfied with saying that the knowability of God is "in the first instance" and "decisively" His own readiness to be known by us, i.e., the readiness grounded in His own being and activity. Later on we shall have to speak of a corresponding readiness of man for this knowledge—for it is certainly a question of our human knowledge of God. If there is not a corresponding readiness of man, there can be no knowability of God—at any rate, not a knowability which will ever be a problem for us. There can be only the knowability of God for Himself, and even this not in a way that it can be the theme of our enquiry. We will have to understand and explain the knowability of God with reference to both God and man, if we are going to understand and explain it properly. But if from the very outset we fix and keep our eyes on this, it must at once become clear to us that the readiness of man cannot be independent. It is a readiness which cannot finally be grounded in itself, i.e. in the nature and activity of man, so that between it and the readiness of God there is a relationship of mutual conditioning, the readiness of man meeting the readiness of God

From Karl Barth, *The Doctrine of God*, vol. II, part 1 of *Church Dogmatics*, trans. T. H. L. Parker, W. B. Johnston, Harold Knight, J. L. M. Haire (Edinburgh, Scotland: T. & T. Clarke, 1957), pp. 63, 65-66, 69, 74, 128, 179-94, 204-14. Reprinted by permission of the publisher.

halfway, so to speak, God and His readiness having to wait, as it were, for the readiness of man in order that together they may constitute the knowability of God which establishes the knowledge of God. . . . In knowing Him, there can be no readiness of man that is finally rounded in itself, as generally there can be no being and activity of another that is finally grounded in itself. If there is this readiness on the side of man, it can have only a borrowed, mediated and subsequent independence. It can be communicated to man only as a capacity and willingness for gratitude and obedience. It can be opened and apportioned to man only from the source of all readiness—the readiness of God Himself, beside which there cannot ultimately be a second. With good reason, therefore, we have to speak first of the readiness of God. And it is not merely the first and decisive readiness. It is the readiness which in principle comprehends, establishes, delimits and determines the readiness of man in the sovereignty of his Lord, Creator, Reconciler and Redeemer. In the last resort therefore, and properly, it is the only readiness of which we have to think when we ask about the knowability of God. . . .

. . . For it is by the grace of God and only by the grace of God that it comes about that God is knowable to us. How do we come to refer ourselves to God Himself and to the fact that He is Himself the truth? It is simply that we have referred ourselves to His revelation, to the fact that He gives Himself to us to be known, thus establishing our knowledge. But we cannot arbitrarily refer ourselves to God's revelation. Not, at any rate, in the way that we do to any other datum of our experience, or to any other real or supposed axiom of our thinking. God's revelation is not in our power, and therefore not at our command. God's revelation takes place among us and for us, in the sphere of our experience and of our thinking. But it has to be seriously accepted that it happens as a movement "from God." It is by the truth itself that in revelation we have to do with the truth itself. And it is only in the truth itself that, summoned and authorised and directed by it, we can effectively refer and appeal to the truth itself. . . .

. . . The fact that God is revealed to us is then grace. Grace is the majesty, the freedom, the undeservedness, the unexpectedness, the newness, the arbitrariness, in which the relationship to God and therefore the possibility of knowing Him is opened up to man by God Himself. Grace is really the orientation in which God sets up an order which did not previously exist, to the power and benefit of which man has no claim, which he has no power to set up, which he has no competence even subsequently to justify, which in its singularity— which corresponds exactly to the singularity of the nature and being of God—he can only recognize and acknowledge as it is actually set up, as it is powerful and effective as a benefit that comes to him. Grace is God's good-pleasure. And it is precisely in God's good-pleasure that the reality of our being with God and of His being with us consists. For it is Jesus Christ who is God's revelation, and the reality of this relationship in Jesus Christ is the work of the divine good-pleasure. God's revelation breaks through the emptiness of the movement of thought which we call our knowledge of God. It gives to this knowledge another side, seen from which it is not self-deception but an event in truth, because it happens by the truth. It makes us those who do not have to do only with themselves but also with God. It provides our knowledge of God with its object. And all this because it is God's good-pleasure. For we, real men, have to do with the real God because the mercy of His good-pleasure comes upon us in all the majesty, freedom, undeservedness, unexpectedness, newness and arbitrariness of grace. . . .

2. The Readiness of Man

. . . We are already agreed on the point that there can be no knowability of God if it is not also to be understood as a readiness of man. This cannot be an independent readiness. It cannot have its final basis in itself (i.e., in the nature and activity of man). It cannot in any sense delimit the readiness of God. There does not exist a relationship of mutual conditionedness between it and the readiness of God. But this does not mean that it is to be denied. "God is knowable" means: "God can be known." In the first part of this section we have understood this ability to consist not only first and decisively, but solely, in the readiness of God, i.e., in the knowability of God bestowed upon us in the grace and mercy of His revelation. But in this readiness of God, which alone comes under consideration in this connexion, the readiness of man is enclosed. With and in the fact that God is ready within Himself to be known by man, man is also ready to know Him. There is no presumption in affirming this. It would be rebellion to deny it. Man's readiness to know God is encompassed and established, delimited and determined by the readiness of God; it is not independent but mediated; subsequent to the readiness of God; called by it out of nothingness into being, out of death into life; utterly dependent of and by itself upon the knowability of God, but in this complete dependence real in the way in which creation generally can only be in its relationship to the Creator. . . .

God is known only by God. We do not know Him, then, in virtue of the views and concepts with which in faith we attempt to respond to His revelation. But we also do not know Him without making use of His permission and obeying His command to undertake this attempt. The success of this undertaking, and therefore the veracity of our human knowledge of God, consists in the fact that our viewing and conceiving is adopted and determined to participation in the truth of God by God Himself in grace.

1. The Hiddenness of God

How far is God known? and how far is God knowable? We have answered these questions in principle in the two previous sections. We may summarise our answer in the statement that God is known by God and by God alone. His revelation is not merely His own readiness to be known, but man's readiness to know Him. God's revelation is, therefore, His knowability. On the ground and in the sphere of this basic answer we now have to give a practical answer—a concrete description of the event between God and man which we call the knowledge of God and which as such is the presupposition, continually to be renewed, of all Christian doctrine, of Church dogmatics and therefore of the preaching of the Church. . . .

. . . [The] fact that in the knowledge of God we have to do in divine certainty with God Himself by God Himself, is one which, as the *terminus a quo* of this event, we must now investigate more closely and define more exactly. We are speaking of the knowledge of God whose subject is God the Father and God the Son through the Holy Spirit. But we men are taken up into this event as secondary, subsequent subjects. Therefore we are not speaking only of an event which takes place on high, in the mystery of the divine Trinity. We are indeed speaking of this event, and the force of anything that is said about the knowledge of God consists in the fact that we speak also and first of this event. But we are now speaking of the revelation of this event on high and therefore of our participation in it. We are speaking of the human knowledge of God on the basis of this revelation and therefore of an event which formally and technically cannot be distinguished from what we call knowledge in other connexions, from human cognition. The fact that it has God not only for its object but also as its origin, and that its primary and proper subject is the Father who knows the Son and the Son who knows the Father in the Holy Spirit, and that it is a sure and perfect and genuine cognition because God is known by God, does not mean either the abrogation, abolition or alteration of human cognition as such, and therefore of its formal and technical characteristics as human cognition. . . .

But what are we saying when we affirm that men can view and conceive God and therefore view and conceive Him after a human manner? When we say this, have we made a statement on human cognitive capacity as such, on a possibility immanent in our viewing and conceiving (i.e., indwelling and proper to it as such)? Does it follow from the fact that we are capable of viewing and conceiving objects in general that in certain circumstances, i.e., presupposing the fact that God reveals Himself to us and therefore makes Himself object to us, we are also capable of viewing and conceiving this object on the basis of the same capacity? Clearly we cannot evade the insight of the whole Early Church and theology that this statement must not be ventured in this sense. If we keep to the fact that God is known only by God, then whatever may be the function of our viewing and conceiving, and however necessary this function may be, it is fixed that we certainly do not know Him by these views and concepts of ours: that is to say, not by their inner power; not in virtue of their own capacity, i.e., of the capacity of human viewing and conceiving as such; not in virtue of a potentiality of our cognition which has perhaps to be actualised by revelation. We definitely cannot deny to this the character and function of an instrument in this event. In the act of the knowledge of God, as in any other cognitive act, we are definitely active as the receivers of images and creators of counter-images. Yet while this is true, it must definitely be contested that our receiving and creating owes its truth to any capacity of our own to be truly recipients and creators in relation to God. It is indeed our own viewing and conceiving. But we ourselves have no capacity for fellowship with God. Between God and us there stands the hiddenness of God, in which He is far from us and foreign to us except as He has of Himself ordained and created fellowship between Himself and us—and this does not happen in the actualising of our capacity, but in the miracle of His good-pleasure. Our viewing as such is certainly capable of receiving images of the divine. And our conceiving as such is certainly capable of creating idolatrous pictures. And both are projections of our own glory. But our viewing and conceiving are not at all capable of grasping God. That is to say, what they grasp as such—as our own viewing and conceiving, as the work of our nature—is as such not God but a reality distinct from God. . . . At this very point it emerges that although the knowledge of God certainly does not come about without our work, it also does not come about through our work, or as the fruit of our work. At this very point the truth breaks imperiously and decisively before us: God is known only by God; God can be known only by God. At this very point, in faith itself, we know God in utter dependence, in pure discipleship and gratitude. At this very point we are finally dissuaded from trusting and confiding in our own capacity and strength. At this very point we can see that our attempt to answer God's revelation with our views and concepts is an attempt undertaken with insufficient means, the work of unprofitable servants, so that we cannot possibly ascribe the success of this attempt and therefore the truth of our knowledge of God to ourselves, i.e., to the capacity of our views and concepts. In faith itself we are forced to say that our knowledge of God begins in all seriousness with the knowledge of the hiddenness of God. . . .

. . . It is in faith, and therefore in the fulfilment of the knowledge of God, and therefore in the real viewing and real conceiving of God, that we can understand the fact that we know, view and conceive God, not as a work of our nature, not as a performance on the basis of our own capacity, but only as a miraculous work of the divine good-pleasure, so that, knowing God, we necessarily know His hiddenness. . . .

. . . We cannot conceive God because we cannot even contemplate Him. He cannot be the object of one of those perceptions to which our concepts, our thought-forms and finally our words and sentences are related. . . .

But this very negation now needs detailed material explanation. The assertion of God's hiddenness (which includes God's invisibility, incomprehensibility and ineffability) tells us that God does not belong to the objects which we can always subjugate to the process of our viewing, conceiving and expressing and therefore our spiritual oversight and control. In contrast to that of all other objects, His nature is not one which in this sense lies in the sphere of our power. God is inapprehensible. . . .

In other words, the lines which we can draw to describe formally and conceptually what we mean when we say "God" cannot be extended so that what is meant is really described and defined; but they continually break apart so that it is not actually described and therefore not defined. In relation to God the means of definition at our disposal are not sufficient to reassure us, when we have applied them to Him, that we have thought what must be thought and said here. The being apprehended by us in thoughts and words is always either not yet or else no longer the being of God. . . .

We thus understand the assertion of the hiddenness of God as the confession of the truth and effectiveness of the sentence of judgment which in the revelation of God in Jesus Christ is pronounced upon man and therefore also upon his viewing and conceiving, dispossessing him of his own possibility of realising the knowledge of the God who encounters him, and leaving him only the knowledge of faith granted to him and demanded of him by the grace of God and therefore only the viewing and conceiving of faith.

But by this same fact we are already impelled to the positive meaning of the statement. Where we really confess God's judgment, we also confess God's grace. The assertion of the hiddenness of God is not, therefore, to be understood as one of despairing resignation, but actually as the *terminus a quo* of our real knowledge of God, as the fundamental and decisive determination, not of our ignorance, but of our cognisance of God. It affirms that our cognisance of God does not begin in ourselves, since it has already begun in God; namely, in God's revelation and in faith to Him. The confession of God's hiddenness is the confession of God's revelation as the beginning of our cognisance of God. Only in a secondary and derived sense is it also a confession of our own incapacity. The emphasis in the confession of God's hiddenness is not primarily that of humility but first and decisively that of gratitude. . . . And because God views and conceives Himself in His Word we know that He is not viewable and conceivable in any other way, and that therefore we are incapable of viewing and conceiving Him of ourselves. . . .

Knowing the true God in His revelation, we apprehend Him in His hiddenness. And just because we do this, we know the true God in His revelation. If He is not always the One whom we of ourselves are unable to view and to conceive, the One whom we know is not the true God in His revelation. Again, He is not this true God if His knowledge does not involve a real human viewing and conceiving, founded and ordered of course by Him alone, and not therefore cancelling His hiddenness. If we deny either the one or the other, we deny His revelation and therefore Himself. . . . In faith itself, and therefore confronted with the true God in His revelation, we cannot deny either the power of God, our impotence, or our power as the gracious gift of God. . . .

2. The Veracity of Man's Knowledge of God

Our next concern is with the *terminus ad quem* of the knowledge of God. We do not understand by this the object as such which is attained by it, although we shall certainly have to speak of its object too—this is inevitable. We understand by the *terminus ad quem* of the knowledge of God, the goal and end, determined by its object, of the event, the movement, the human action which we call the knowledge of God; the limit by which as such it is separated from its object as such, but by which it is also united with it.

. . . A circular course is involved because God is known by God, and only by God; because even as an action undertaken and performed by man, knowledge of God is objectively and subjectively both instituted by God Himself and led to its end by Him; because God the Father and the Son by the Holy Spirit is its primary and proper subject and object. If it is also a human undertaking and action, if as such it also arrives at its goal, this is in consequence of the fact that God does not wish to know Himself without Himself giving us a part in this event in the grace of His revelation. . . .

. . . For without the grace of His revelation, God is definitely not an object of human cognition, and definitely no object of human cognition is God. It is by God's revelation that we know God as the One who is absolutely perfect and self-sufficient, as the One whose being is absolutely self-determined and self-fulfilled and therefore self-enclosed, because in His being and for the felicity of His being He does not need another in the knowledge of whom He must first be confirmed and verified as the One He is. It is by God's revelation that we therefore know God as the One who only by His revelation, as the free good-pleasure and free activity of His overflowing love, can be the object of our cognition, the object of our substantiation and acceptance. There is not another necessity, that it must be so, or even another possibility, that it can be so. God reveals Himself to us in Jesus Christ as the One who does not owe us Himself, but has bestowed Himself upon us. If we have to do with Him, the possibility and necessity on the basis of which this is so are grounded only on the fact that He wills to have these dealings with us. We can therefore describe God as an object of human cognition, and an object of human cognition as God, only on the assumption that it has pleased and does please God—in an earlier connexion we spoke of a divine "encroachment"—to make Himself the object of our cognition. Just as we ourselves have no capacity for fellowship with God and therefore no capacity to view and conceive God, and, in relation to Him, to be true receivers and creators and therefore subjects of this knowledge, so there is in itself neither a necessity nor even a possibility that God must or can be present as the object of our viewing and conceiving. God is the One who is to and by and in Himself. On the basis of His revelation we shall have to say this with quite another emphasis and weight than we could say it on the basis of a philosophical definition of the absolute. As such, God does not have to be the object of our cognition. As such, He cannot be it at all. If, in spite of this, He is, what is revealed in this fact is only the exuberant freedom of the love in which He is who He is; not a necessity, on the basis of which He has to be this, or even the possibility, on the basis of which He can be. In His self-revelation as Father, Son and Holy Spirit we can see the fact that He is the object of our cognition; we can find Him as the One who in the depths of His being is in fact none other than the One who loves us, and therefore bestows Himself upon us, positing Himself as the object of our cognition. . . .

With this as a starting-point, we must now consider the success of the human undertaking to view and conceive God, and therefore the truth or veracity of our human knowledge of God. The success of this undertaking, if success if attained, obviously consists in the veracity of the human knowledge of God, namely, in the fact that, knowing God, we do not have to do with something else or someone else, but validly, compulsorily, unassailably and trustworthily with God Himself. And beyond that, it consists in the fact that we do not have to do with Him only in a loose way, or at random, or with the threat of mistakes from unknown sources, or with the reservation that in reality everything might be quite different, but in a way which is right, which formally as well as materially cannot be separated from the matter itself, and therefore in this respect, too, validly, compulsorily, unassailably and trustworthily. . . .

The veracity of our knowledge of God is the veracity of His revelation. This is the statement which we now have to expound. The truth of the revelation of God consists first and decisively in the fact that it is His, God's revelation. It is not someone or something else which reveals God, but God reveals Himself. . . . God's revelation is authentic information about God because it is first-hand information, because in it God is His own witness and teacher. The fact that we have to do with Him—no, that He in His revelation has to do with us—makes our knowledge of God true. Whatever we may always have to say about its natural limitations, and whatever critical prudence and frankness we may have to bring to its attainment, priority must be given to the fact that it is correct knowledge of God because the revelation from which it springs and to which it is related is God's own revelation and therefore correct. Any closer definition, any reservation, any caveat can only follow the affirmation that with our knowledge of God we do not draw from our own source or an alien source, but directly from the well of God Himself; that it is pure praise and thanksgiving to the Father who Himself has represented Himself to us in the Son by the Holy Spirit. For this reason it is true knowledge; for this reason our undertaking to view and conceive Him is an undertaking that succeeds; for this reason we speak, as we believe, in the certainty that we do not speak in vain, but, with a good conscience before ourselves and everyman, declare the truth and nothing but the truth.

. . . And when we say this, we are saying that the claim made upon us by His revelation does not demand anything impossible, and therefore that it is not an impotent and ineffectual claim. If God commands, it is so. And in the present context this means that, if He will have it so, we shall think of Him with what are certainly (from our standpoint) impotent views and concepts, and that we shall speak of Him what (again from our standpoint) are certainly impotent words. It means that God Himself, with His will to reveal Himself and therefore His claim upon us, takes our place, and therefore that, with His power to reveal Himself, He does not ignore or eliminate but fills up the void of our impotence to view and conceive Him. Our inability to perform by our action what is demanded of us is not at all His inability to cause what is demanded to happen by our action. What we of ourselves cannot do, He can do through us. . . . This indwelling does not involve a magical transformation of man, or a supernatural enlargement of his capacity, so that now he can do what before he could not do. He cannot do it afterwards any more than he could do before. But he is taken up by the grace of God and determined to participation in the veracity of the revelation of God. . . .

. . . That God in His grace will take up His dwelling in the confines of our thinking and speaking cannot mean that He has surrendered Himself to us as our prisoner. He dwells where our thinking and speaking about Him take place in obedience: in obedience to His grace, which is *His* grace. . . .

The decisive thing about the veracity of human knowledge of God is undoubtedly said when we remember the veracity of the revelation of God. The human knowledge of God becomes and is true because God is truly God in His revelation; because His revelation is true as such; because in it he truly claims human thinking and speaking; because in it He truly justifies human thinking and speaking; because by it He upholds us as those who think of Him and speak of Him in humility before Him. . . . The grace of the revelation of God, which we came to know as the *terminus a quo* of our knowledge of God, is therefore also its *terminus ad quem.*

For Further Reading

Barth, Karl. *Against the Stream: Shorter Post-War Writings, 1946–1952.* Ed. R. H. Smith. Trans. E. M. Delacour and Stanley Godman. London: SCM Press, 1954.

———. *Church Dogmatics: A Selection.* Ed. Helmut Gollwitzer. Trans. G. W. Bromiley. New York: Harper & Row, 1962.

———. *Dogmatics in Outline.* Trans. G. T. Thomson. New York: Harper & Row, 1959.

———. *Epistle to the Romans.* London: SCM Press, 1933.

———. *Evangelical Theology: An Introduction.* Trans. Grover Foley. New York: Holt, Rinehart & Winston, 1963.

———. *The Knowledge of God and the Service of God.* Trans. J. L. M. Haire and Ian Henderson. London: Hodder & Stoughton, 1938.

Casalis, Georges. *Portrait of Karl Barth.* New York: Doubleday, 1963.

Torrance, Thomas F. *Karl Barth: An Introduction to His Early Theology, 1910–1931.* London: SCM Press, 1962.

II

GENERAL
REVELATION

Anselm of Canterbury

(1033–1109)

S AINT ANSELM WAS ONE OF THE BEST-KNOWN THINKERS IN medieval philosophy and theology. Born in 1033, Anselm became a Benedictine monk at the Abbey of Bec in Normandy, where he later became prior (1063). In 1093 he was elected archbishop of Canterbury, a post he held until his death in 1109.

There was no sharp dividing line between theology and philosophy, between faith and reason, for Anselm. Like Augustine, upon whose work he relied heavily, he sought to provide rational support for the teachings of Christianity, which he accepted on faith. He was certain that faith *and* reason, rightly employed, led to the same conclusions. Anselm's intellectual interests were thus theological, and his philosophy was that of a firmly committed believer seeking to understand his faith. He believed that for those who are capable of it, rigorous reasoning is an integral part of faith; he was also concerned to use reason to demonstrate the truth of Christianity to non-believers. Although Anselm is said by some to have offered "proofs" of God's existence, they are not necessarily proofs such as would convince an adamant non-believer, apart from some dawning predisposition to faith. The arguments are best understood as "demonstrations" rather than "proofs" in a narrow sense.

Initially, in the *Monologium* Anselm develops two arguments for God's existence, based upon our experience of the world. (1) The *proof from degrees:* We compare, for example, degrees of the good, such as better and worse, greater and lesser. We also recognize degrees or levels of being, such as inorganic, plant, animal, and human. In order to recognize differences in degree, there has to be an absolute point of comparison—a greatest good, a highest and most perfect Being. This most perfect, highest Being and absolute Good is God. (2) The *proof from existence:* Whatever is must have an adequate cause for its existence. Something cannot come from nothing. Therefore, everything must be either self-caused or caused by something other than itself. Something cannot be self-caused because, before it is, it is nothing. Therefore, there must be an uncaused cause of all things, and this is God.

However, Anselm was not satisfied with these arguments, because he thought them debatable. He sought a more sophisticated argument, one which relied only upon rational thought itself. He developed such a demonstration in the *Proslogium,* the *a priori* ontological argument. It reflects the Augustinian idea that God is that Being greater than which none can be conceived. Summarized, the ontological argument proceeds as follows:

A. By "God" we mean that Being no greater than which can be thought.
B. A Being that exists only as an idea in our minds is of necessity a lesser Being than one that exists in reality, because an existing Being is clearly greater than a nonexistent Being.
C. Therefore, because the idea of God includes supreme greatness, God must exist in reality, not just as an idea.

Existence, in other words, is a property of God in the same way that three interior angles and three sides are properties of a triangle.

Gaunilon, another Benedictine monk, took up the case of the "fool" whom Anselm had rather summarily dismissed in chapter 2 of the *Proslogium.* Gaunilon did not wish to deny God's existence, which he, like Anselm, accepted on faith, but he did set out to show that Anselm had not constructed an adequate proof.

On behalf of the "fool" Gaunilon made two arguments. First, the fool could not form the idea that God is that being none greater than which can be thought, because there is nothing upon which to base such an idea. Anselm himself argues that God is unique among all realities. Second, said Gaunilon, we often think of things that do not exist, such as a perfect island. We can think it; it does not necessarily exist.

Anselm responded to both, in essence repeating his argument. We *do* form "none greater than" concepts every time we compare degrees of something such as goodness and move upward to the absolute, as absolute goodness or perfection. (Notice here the resemblance to the arguments in the *Monologium.*) In the second place, Gaunilon's analogy with the perfect island shows that he has missed an essential point. We can move from an idea to the necessity of its existence in one case only, a Being whose nonexistence cannot be thought. An island does not have to be; its existence is contingent. The analogy does not hold up because God is necessary rather than contingent being.

* * *

THE ONTOLOGICAL ARGUMENT

In this brief work the author aims at proving in a single argument the existence of God, and whatsoever we believe of God.—The difficulty of the task.—The author writes in the person of one who contemplates God, and seeks to understand what he believes. To this work he had given this title: Faith Seeking Understanding. He finally named it Proslogium,—that is, A Discourse.

After I had published, at the solicitous entreaties of certain brethren, a brief work (the *Monologium*) as an example of meditation on the grounds of faith, in the person of one who investigates, in a course of silent reasoning with himself, matters of which he is ignorant; considering that this book was knit together by the linking of many arguments, I began to ask myself whether there might be found a single argument which would require no other for its proof than itself alone; and alone would suffice to demonstrate that God truly exists, and that there is a supreme good requiring nothing else, which all other things require for their existence and well-being; and whatever we believe regarding the divine Being.

Although I often and earnestly directed my thought to this end, and at some times that which I sought seemed to be just within my reach, while again it wholly evaded my mental vision, at last in despair I was about to cease, as if from the search for a thing which could not be found. But when I wished to exclude this thought altogether, lest, by busying my mind to no purpose, it should keep me from other thoughts, in which I might be successful; then more and more, though I was unwilling and shunned it, it began to force itself upon me, with a kind of importunity. So, one day, when I was exceedingly wearied with resisting its importunity, in the very conflict of my thoughts, the proof of which I had despaired offered itself, so that I eagerly embraced the thoughts which I was strenuously repelling.

Thinking, therefore, that what I rejoiced to have found, would, if put in writing, be welcome to some readers, of this very matter, and of some others, I have written the following treatise, in the person of one who strives to lift his mind to the contemplation of God, and seeks to understand what he believes. . . .

. . . Teach me to seek thee, and reveal thyself to me, when I seek thee, for I cannot seek thee, except thou teach me, nor find thee, except thou reveal thyself. Let me seek thee in longing, let me long for thee in seeking; let me find thee in love, and love thee in finding. Lord, I acknowledge and I thank thee that thou hast created me in this thine image, in order that I may be mindful of thee, may conceive of thee, and love thee; but that image has been so consumed and wasted away by vices, and obscured by the smoke of wrong-doing, that it cannot achieve that for which it was made, except thou renew it, and create it anew. I do not endeavor, O Lord, to penetrate thy sublimity, for in no wise do I compare my understanding with that; but I long to understand in some degree thy truth, which my heart believes and loves. For I do not seek to understand that I may believe, but I believe in order to understand. For this also I believe,—that unless I believed, I should not understand. . . .

Truly there is a God, although the fool hath said in his heart, There is no God.

And so, Lord, do thou, who dost give understanding to faith, give me, so far as thou knowest it to be profitable, to understand that thou art as we believe; and that thou art that which we believe. And, indeed, we believe that thou art a being than which nothing greater can be conceived. Or is there no such nature, since the fool hath said in his heart, there is no God? (Psalms xiv. I). But, at any rate, this very fool, when he hears of this being of which I speak—a being than which nothing greater can be conceived—understands what he hears, and what he understands is in his understanding; although he does not understand it to exist.

For, it is one thing for an object to be in the understanding, and another to understand that the object exists. When a painter first conceives of what he will afterwards perform, he has it in his understanding, but he does not yet understand it to be, because he has not yet performed it. But after he has made the painting, he both has it in his understanding, and he understands that it exists, because he has made it.

Hence, even the fool is convinced that something exists in the understanding, at least, than which nothing greater can be conceived. For, when he hears of this, he understands it. And whatever is understood, exists in the understanding. And assuredly that, than which nothing greater can be conceived, cannot exist in the understanding alone. For, suppose it exists in the understanding alone: then it can be conceived to exist in reality; which is greater. . . .

God cannot be conceived not to exist.—God is that, than which nothing greater can be conceived.—That which can be conceived not to exist is not God.

And it assuredly exists so truly, that it cannot be conceived not to exist. For, it is possible to conceive of a being which cannot be conceived not to exist; and this is greater than one which can be conceived not to exist. Hence, if that, than which nothing greater can be conceived, can be conceived not to exist, it is not that, than which nothing greater can be conceived. But this is an irreconcilable contradiction. There is, then, so truly a being than which nothing greater can be conceived to exist, that it cannot even be conceived not to exist; and this being thou art, O Lord, our God.

So truly, therefore, dost thou exist, O Lord, my God, that thou canst not be conceived not to exist; and rightly. For, if a mind could conceive of a being better than thee, the creature would rise above the Creator; and this is most absurd. And, indeed, whatever else there is, except thee alone, can be conceived not to exist. To thee alone, therefore, it belongs to exist more truly than all other beings, and hence in a higher degree than all others. For, whatever else exists does not exist so truly, and hence in a less degree it belongs to it to exist. Why, then, has the fool said in his heart, there is no God (Psalms xiv. I), since it is so evident, to a rational mind, that thou dost exist in the highest degree of all? Why, except that he is dull and a fool? . . .

How the fool has said in his heart what cannot be conceived.—A thing may be conceived in two ways: (1) when the word signifying it is conceived; (2) when the thing itself is understood. As far as the word goes, God can be conceived not to exist; in reality he cannot.

But how has the fool said in his heart what he could not conceive; or how is it that he could not conceive what he said in his heart? since it is the same to say in the heart, and to conceive.

But, if really, nay, since really, he both conceived, because he said in his heart; and did not say in his heart, because he could not conceive; there is more than one way in which a thing is said in the heart or conceived. For, in one sense, an object is conceived, when the word signifying it is conceived; and in another, when the very entity, which the object is, is understood.

In the former sense, then, God can be conceived not to exist; but in the latter, not at all. For no one who understands what fire and water are can conceive fire to be water, in accordance with the nature of the facts themselves, although this is possible according to the words. So, then, no one who understands what God is can conceive that God does not exist; although he says these words in his heart, either without any, or with some foreign, signification. For, God is that than which a greater cannot be conceived. And he who thoroughly understands this, assuredly understands that this being so truly exists, that not even in concept can it be non-existent. Therefore, he who understands that God so exists, cannot conceive that he does not exist.

I thank thee, gracious Lord, I thank thee; because what I formerly believed by thy bounty, I now so understand by thine illumination, that if I were unwilling to believe that thou dost exist, I should not be able not to understand this to be true. . . .

God is whatever it is better to be than not to be; and he, as the only self-existent being, creates all things from nothing.

What art thou, then, Lord God, than whom nothing greater can be conceived? But what art thou, except that which, as the highest of all beings, alone exists through itself, and creates all other things from nothing? For, whatever is not this is less than a thing which can be conceived of. But this cannot be conceived of thee. What good, therefore, does the supreme God lack, through which every good is? Therefore, thou art just, truthful, blessed, and whatever it is better to be than not to be. For it is better to be just than not just; better to be blessed than not blessed. . . .

He is greater than can be conceived.

Therefore, O Lord, thou art not only that than which a greater cannot be conceived, but thou art a being greater than can be conceived. For, since it can be conceived that there is such a being, if thou art not this very being, a greater than thou can be conceived. But this is impossible.

For Further Reading

Hartshorne, Charles. *Anselm's Discovery: A Re-examination of the Ontological Proof of God's Existence.* LaSalle, Ill.: Open Court Publishing Co., 1965.

Hopkins, Jasper. *A Companion to the Study of Saint Anselm.* Minneapolis: University of Minnesota Press, 1972.

Saint Thomas Aquinas

(c. 1225–1274)

BORN NEAR NAPLES, THOMAS AQUINAS SEEMED DESTINED almost from the beginning for a career in the church. Initially, he became a Benedictine oblate, as had Saint Anselm. After his father's death, against his family's wishes, he joined the Dominican Order. He studied and taught at several schools until he joined the University of Paris as a fully accredited member of the theology faculty in 1257. He taught there only two years, spending the next ten years at various Dominican monasteries around Rome. He returned to the University of Paris from 1268 to 1272; then the Dominicans recalled him to Italy and the University of Naples. He taught there for only a year, being forced into retirement by failing health. He died in 1274 en route to a church council. Most of his voluminous writing was done between 1252 and 1273, his most active learning and teaching years. He produced several large theological treatises and recorded disputations on theological and philosophical problems, various biblical commentaries, commentaries on the works of Aristotle and other philosophers, plus miscellaneous letters, sermons, and shorter treatises.

Aquinas perfected the "scholastic method," the attempt to develop a coherent system of traditional thought through the process of logical deduction. The emphasis is on the method and on rational coherence rather than on attaining truly novel insight. The method itself is disputational or dialectical, emphasizing genuine engagement between opposing points of view.

Aquinas taught and wrote in both theology and philosophy, integrating without confusing the two disciplines. He delineated their boundaries and proper roles clearly: Philosophy is based upon principles discovered by reason. When knowledge of God is concerned, philosophy begins, as does all reasoning, with sense experience and works upward to God. Theology, on the other hand, begins with faith and consists in the rational ordering and interpretation of principles received via revelation and held to be authoritative. Matters necessary for salvation are given via revelation, according to Thomas; some such matters could not be discovered by reason at all, while others, discoverable by reason, are revealed to ensure their availability. Ultimately, however, there can be no conflict between philosophy and theology, between reason and faith. Both the data of nature and the principles of reasoning, as well as revelation, come from God, and there is no difference in principle between the reality toward which each is oriented. Reason and faith thus supplement each other. They do not conflict, nor can one supplant the other.

In the main, Thomas' philosophy is a rethinking of Aristotelianism along lines that show its coherence with Christian faith. He does with Aristotle much the same thing as Anselm does with the philosophy of Plato, through the synthesis that Augustine had brought about between medieval Christianity and Platonic thought.

Thomas' well known "five proofs of the existence of God" are all *a posteriori*; that is, they begin with experience. Both cosmological and teleological proofs are included. Thomas was particularly concerned to reject two views. He rejects an anti-intellectual fideism that claims God cannot be known but only believed in by "blind" faith. On the other hand, he does not support Anselm's analytic argument that the existence of God is self-evident once we understand what is meant by the term "God." In lieu of both of these, he teaches that the existence of God can be demonstrated conclusively on the basis of data found in the natural world, and he does this in the five proofs. The style in which these are discussed provides us with a good illustration of his disputational method.

The first two of the five proofs are of parallel form: We know there is (1) motion and (2) causality. In order to avoid an infinite regress, an absurdity which reason will not tolerate, there must be an unmoved mover or an uncaused cause, and this is God. The third proof rests on a similar need for necessary as opposed to contingent being. The fourth proof argues in a vein reminiscent of Anselm's *Monologium* discussion of degrees of goodness. The last is a classic argument from the observation of order in the universe, a statement we find amplified in William Paley's argument from design.

* * *

THE COSMOLOGICAL ARGUMENT

Because the chief aim of sacred doctrine is to teach the knowledge of God not only as He is in Himself, but also as He is the beginning of things and their last end, and especially of rational creatures, as is clear from what has been already said, therefore, in our endeavor to expound this science, we shall treat: (1) of God; (2) of the rational creature's movement towards God; (3) of Christ Who as man is our way to God.

In treating of God there will be a threefold division:—

For we shall consider (1) whatever concerns the divine essence. (2) Whatever concerns the distinctions of Persons. (3) Whatever concerns the procession of creatures from Him.

Concerning the divine essence, we must consider:—

(1) Whether God exists? (2) The manner of His existence, or, rather what is not the manner of His existence. (3) Whatever concerns His operations—namely, His knowledge, will, power.

Concerning the first, there are three points of inquiry:—

(1) Whether the proposition God *exists* is self-evident? (2) Whether it is demonstrable? (3) Whether God exists?

First Article
Whether the Existence of God Is Self-Evident?

We proceed thus to the First Article:—

Objection 1. It seems that the existence of God is self-evident. For those things are said to be self-evident to us the knowledge of which exists naturally in us, as we can see in regard to first principles. But as Damascene says, *the knowledge of God is naturally implanted in all.* Therefore the existence of God is self-evident.

Obj. 2. Further, those things are said to be self-evident which are known as soon as the terms are known, which the Philosopher says is true of the first principles of demonstration. Thus, when the nature of a whole and of a part is known, it is at once recognized that every whole is greater than its part. But as soon as the signification of the name *God* is understood, it is at once seen that God exists. For by this name is signified that thing than which nothing greater can be conceived. But

From *Basic Writings of Saint Thomas Aquinas*, vol. 1, trans. and ed. Anton C. Pegis (New York: Random House, 1945), pp. 19-24. Copyright © 1977 by Anton C. Pegis. Reprinted by permission of the A. C. Pegis Estate.

that which exists actually and mentally is greater than that which exists only mentally. Therefore, since as soon as the name *God* is understood it exists mentally, it also follows that it exists actually. Therefore the proposition *God exists* is self-evident.

Obj. 3. Further, the existence of truth is self-evident. For whoever denies the existence of truth grants that truth does not exist: and, if truth does not exist, then the proposition *Truth does not exist* is true: and if there is anything true, there must be truth. But God is truth itself: I am the way, the truth, and the life (*Jo.* xiv. 6). Therefore *God exists* is self-evident.

On the contrary, No one can mentally admit the opposite of what is self-evident, as the Philosopher states concerning the first principles of demonstration. But the opposite of the proposition *God is* can be mentally admitted: *The fool said in his heart, There is no God* (Ps. lii. 1). Therefore, that God exists is not self-evident.

I answer that, A thing can be self-evident in either of two ways: on the one hand, self-evident in itself, though not to us; on the other, self-evident in itself, and to us. A proposition is self-evident because the predicate is included in the essence of the subject: e.g., *Man is an animal,* for animal is contained in the essence of man. If, therefore, the essence of the predicate and subject be known to all, the proposition will be self-evident to all; as is clear with regard to the first principles of demonstration, the terms of which are certain common notions that no one is ignorant of, such as being and non-being, whole and part, and the like. If, however, there are some to whom the essence of the predicate and subject is unknown, the proposition will be self-evident in itself, but not to those who do not know the meaning of the predicate and subject of the proposition. Therefore, it happens, as Boethius says, that there are some notions of the mind which are common and self-evident only to the learned, as that incorporeal substances are not in space. Therefore I say that this proposition, *God exists,* of itself is self-evident, for the predicate is the same as the subject, because God is His own existence as will be hereafter shown. Now because we do not know the essence of God, the proposition is not self-evident to us, but needs to be demonstrated by things that are more known to us, though less known in their nature—namely, by His effects.

Reply Obj. 1. To know that God exists in a general and confused way is implanted in us by nature, inasmuch as God is man's beatitude. For man naturally desires happiness, and what is naturally desired by man is naturally known by him. This, however, is not to know absolutely that God exists; just as to know that someone is approaching is not the same as to know that Peter is approaching, even though it is Peter who is approaching; for there are many who imagine that man's perfect good, which is happiness, consists in riches, and others in pleasures, and others in something else.

Reply Obj. 2. Perhaps not everyone who hears this name *God* understands it to signify something than which nothing greater can be thought, seeing that some have believed God to be a body. Yet, granted that everyone understands that by this name *God* is signified something than which nothing greater can be thought, nevertheless, it does not therefore follow that he understands that what the name signifies exists actually, but only that it exists mentally. Nor can it be argued that it actually exists, unless it be admitted that there actually exists something than which nothing greater can be thought; and this precisely is not admitted by those who hold that God does not exist.

Reply Obj. 3. The existence of truth in general is self-evident, but the existence of a Primal Truth is not self-evident to us.

Second Article
Whether It Can Be Demonstrated That God Exists?

We proceed thus to the Second Article:—

Objection 1. It seems that the existence of God cannot be demonstrated. For it is an article of faith that God exists. But what is of faith cannot be demonstrated, because a demonstration produces scientific knowledge, whereas faith is of the unseen, as is clear from the Apostle (*Heb.* xi. 1). Therefore it cannot be demonstrated that God exists.

Obj. 2. Further, essence is the middle term of demonstration. But we cannot know in what God's essence consists, but solely in what it does not consist, as Damascene says. Therefore we cannot demonstrate that God exists.

Obj. 3. Further, if the existence of God were demonstrated, this could only be from His effects. But His effects are not proportioned to Him, since He is infinite and His effects are finite, and between the finite and infinite there is no proportion. Therefore, since a cause cannot be demonstrated by an effect not proportioned to it, it seems that the existence of God cannot be demonstrated.

On the contrary, The Apostle says: *The invisible things of Him are clearly seen, being understood by the things that are made* (*Rom.* i. 20). But this would not be unless the existence of God could be demonstrated through the things that are made; for the first thing we must know of anything is, whether it exists.

I answer that, Demonstration can be made in two ways: One is through the cause, and is called *propter quid,* and this is to argue from what is prior absolutely. The other is through the effect, and is called a demonstration *quia;* this is to argue from what is prior relatively only to us. When an effect is better known to us that its cause, from the effect we proceed to the knowledge of the cause. And from every effect the existence of its proper cause can be demonstrated, so long as its effects are better known to us; because, since every effect depends upon its cause, if the effect exists, the cause must pre-exist. Hence the existence of God, in so far as it is not self-evident to us, can be demonstrated from those of His effects which are known to us.

Reply Obj. 1. The existence of God and other like truths about God, which can be known by natural reason, are not articles of faith, but are preambles to the articles; for faith presupposes natural knowledge, even as grace pre-supposes nature and perfection the perfectible. Nevertheless, there is nothing to prevent a man, who cannot grasp a proof, from accepting, as a matter of faith, something which in itself is capable of being scientifically known and demonstrated.

Reply. Obj. 2. When the existence of a cause is demonstrated from an effect, this effect takes the place of the definition of the cause in proving the cause's existence. This is especially the case in regard to God, because, in order to prove the existence of anything, it is necessary to accept as a middle term the meaning of the name, and not its essence, for the question of its essence follows on the question of its existence. Now the names given to God are derived from His effects, as will be later shown. Consequently, in demonstrating the existence of God from His effects, we may take for the middle term the meaning of the name *God.*

Reply Obj. 3. From effects not proportioned to the cause no perfect knowledge of that cause can be obtained. Yet from every effect the existence of the cause can be clearly demonstrated, and so we can demonstrate the existence of God from His effects; though from them we cannot know God perfectly as He is in His essence.

Third Article
Whether God Exists?

We proceed thus to the Third Article:—

Objection 1. It seems that God does not exist; because if one of two contraries be infinite, the other would be altogether destroyed. But the name God means that He is infinite goodness. If, therefore, God existed, there would be no evil discoverable; but there is evil in the world. Therefore God does not exist.

Obj. 2. Further, it is superfluous to suppose that what can be accounted for by a few principles has been produced by many. But it seems that everything we see in the world can be accounted for by other principles, supposing God did not exist. For all natural things can be reduced to one principle, which is nature; and all voluntary things can be reduced to one principle, which is human reason, or will. Therefore there is no need to suppose God's existence.

On the contrary, It is said in the person of God: I am Who am (Exod. iii. 14).

I answer that, The existence of God can be proved in five ways.

The first and more manifest way is the argument from motion. It is certain, and evident to our senses, that in the world some things are in motion. Now whatever is moved is moved by another, for nothing can be moved except it is in potentiality to that towards which it is moved; whereas a thing moves inasmuch as it is in act. For motion is nothing else than the reduction of something from potentiality to actuality. But nothing can be reduced from potentiality to actuality, except by something in a state of actuality. Thus that which is actually hot, as fire, makes wood, which is potentially hot, to be actually hot, and thereby moves and changes it. Now it is not possible that the same thing should be at once in actuality and potentiality in the same respect, but only in different respects. For what is actually hot cannot simultaneously be potentially hot; but it is simultaneously potentially cold. It is therefore impossible that in the same respect and in the same way a thing should be both mover and moved, i.e., that it should move itself. Therefore, whatever is moved, then this also must needs be moved by another, and that by another again. But this cannot go on to infinity, because there would be no first mover, and, consequently, no other mover seeing that subsequent movers move only inasmuch as they are moved by the first mover; as the staff moves only because it is moved by the hand. Therefore it is necessary to arrive at a first mover, moved by no other; and this everyone understands to be God.

The second way is from the nature of efficient cause. In the world of sensible things we find there is an order of efficient causes. There is no case known (neither is it, indeed, possible) in which a thing is found to be the efficient cause of itself; for so it would be prior to itself, which is impossible. Now in efficient causes it is not possible to go on to infinity, because in all efficient causes following in order, the first is the cause of the intermediate cause, and the intermediate is the cause of the ultimate cause, whether the intermediate cause be several, or one only. Now to take away the cause is to take away the effect. Therefore, if there be no first cause among efficient causes, there will be no ultimate, nor any intermediate, cause. But if in efficient causes it is possible to go on to infinity, there will be no first efficient cause, neither will there be an ultimate effect, nor any intermediate efficient causes; all of which is plainly false. Therefore it is necessary to admit a first efficient cause, to which everyone gives the name God.

The third way is taken from possibility and necessity, and runs thus. We find in nature things that are possible to be and not to be, since they are found to be generated, and to be corrupted, and consequently, it is possible for them to be and not to be. But it is impossible for these always to exist, for that which can not-be at some time is not. Therefore, if everything can not-be, then at one time there was nothing in existence. Now if this were true, even now there would be nothing in existence, because that which does not exist begins to exist only through something already existing. Therefore if at one time nothing was in existence, it would have been impossible for anything to have begun to exist; and thus even now nothing would be in existence—which is absurd. Therefore, not all beings are merely possible, but there must exist something the existence of which is necessary. But every necessary thing either has its necessity caused by another, or not. Now it is impossible to go on to infinity in necessary things which have their necessity caused by another, as has been already proved in regard to efficient causes. Therefore we cannot but admit the existence of some being having of itself its own necessity, and not receiving it from another, but rather causing in others their necessity. This all men speak of as God.

The fourth way is taken from the gradation to be found in things. Among beings there are some more and some less good, true, noble, and the like. But more and less are predicated of different things according as they resemble in their different ways something which is the maximum, as a thing is said to be hotter according as it more nearly resembles that which is hottest so that there is something which is truest, something best, something noblest, and, consequently, something which is most being, for those things that are greatest in truth are greatest in being, as it is written in Metaph. ii. Now the maximum in any genus is the cause of all in that genus, as fire, which is the maximum of heat, is the cause of all hot things, as is said in the same book. Therefore, there must also be something which is to all beings the cause of their being, goodness, and every other perfection; and this we call God.

The fifth way is taken from the governance of the world. We see that things which lack knowledge, such as natural bodies, act for an end, and this is evident from their acting always, or nearly always, in the same way, so as to obtain the best result. Hence it is plain that they achieve their end, not fortuitously, but designedly. Now whatever lacks knowledge cannot move towards an end, unless it be directed by some being endowed with knowledge and intelligence; as the arrow is directed by the archer. Therefore some intelligent being exists by whom all natural things are directed to their end; and this being we call God.

Reply Obj. 1. As Augustine says: *Since God is the highest good, He would not allow any evil to exist in His works, unless His omnipotence and goodness were such as to bring good even out of evil.* This is part of the infinite goodness of God, that He should allow evil to exist, and out of it produce good.

Reply Obj. 2. Since nature works for a determinate end under the direction of a higher agent, whatever is done by nature must be traced back to God as to its first cause. So likewise whatever is done voluntarily must be traced back to some higher cause other than human reason and will, since these can change and fail; for all things that are changeable and capable of defect must be traced back to an immovable and self-necessary first principle, as has been shown.

For Further Reading

Thomas Aquinas, St. *Basic Writings of St. Thomas Aquinas.* 3 vols. Trans. and ed. Anton C. Pegis. New York: Random House, 1945.

Copleston, Frederick C. *Aquinas.* Baltimore: Penguin Books, 1963.

Gilson, Etienne. *The Spirit of Thomism.* New York: P. J. Kennedy, 1964.

Maritain, Jacques. *The Angelic Doctor: The Life and Thought of St. Thomas Aquinas.* Trans. J. F. Scanlon. London: Sheed and Ward, 1948.

10   William Paley

(1743–1805)

WILLIAM PALEY WAS AN ENGLISH THEOLOGIAN AND ethicist. He studied at Christ's College, Cambridge, and was elected Fellow of the College in 1766, where he taught for the next nine years. A devout believer, Paley was ordained a priest in the established Church of England in 1767. Following his marriage he left Cambridge and thereafter held a succession of church offices, the highest of which was archdeacon of Carlisle.

Paley wrote two books in which he addressed the topic of the existence of God: *A View of the Evidences of Christianity* and, later, *Natural Theology*. His "watchmaker" argument may well be the best known of the various philosophical "proofs" of God's existence. It goes like this: Any reasonable person, observing the meticulous design of a watch, infers the existence of a designer/artisan who made it. Likewise, observation of the order and design of the world leads one to infer the existence of a world designer, that is, God. Paley understands that the natural world is full of evidences of this order, the human eye and the complexities of the insect world providing the most persuasive examples.

Not only does observation of the natural world allow us to infer that God is; it gives us some knowledge of God's character. Such an Orderer of the world clearly has a mind and is therefore obviously personal. Most of the arrangements of the world are beneficial, so the Orderer must be good; this is further borne out by the existence of pleasure itself. Truly, as Paley experienced the world in which he lived, "the Heavens declared the glory of God and the firmament showed God's handiwork."

* * *

THE TELEOLOGICAL ARGUMENT

In crossing a heath, suppose I pitched my foot against a stone and were asked how the stone came to be there. I might possibly answer that for anything I knew to the contrary it had lain there forever; nor would it, perhaps, be very easy to show the absurdity of this answer. But suppose I had found a *watch* upon the ground, and it should be inquired how the watch happened to be in that place, I should hardly think of the answer which I had before given, that for anything I knew the watch might have always been there. Yet why should not this answer serve for the watch as well as for the stone? Why is it not as admissible in the second case as in the first? For this reason, and for no other, namely, that when we come to inspect the watch, we perceive—what we could not discover in the stone—that its several parts are framed and put together for a purpose, e.g., that they are so formed and adjusted as to produce motion, and that motion so regulated as to point out the hour of the day; that if the different parts had been differently shaped from what they are, or of a different size from what they are, or placed after any other manner or in any other order, than that in which they are placed, either no motion at all would have been carried on in the machine, or none which would have answered the use that is now served by it. . . . This mechanism being observed—it requires indeed an examination of the instrument, and perhaps some previous knowledge of the subject, to perceive and understand it; but being once, as we have said, observed and understood—the inference, we think, is inevitable, that the watch must have had a maker—that there must have existed, at some time and at some place or other, an artificer or artificers who formed it for the purpose which we find it actually to answer; who comprehended its construction and designed its use.

I. Nor would it, I apprehend, weaken the conclusion, that we had never seen a watch made—that we had never known an artist capable of making one—that we were altogether incapable of executing such a piece of workmanship ourselves, or of understanding in what manner it was performed; . . . Ignorance of this kind exalts our opinion of the unseen and unknown artist's skill, if he be unseen and unknown, but raises no doubt in our minds of the existence and agency of such an artist. . . .

From William Paley, *Natural Theology* (Boston: Gould and Lincoln, 1854), pp. 9-21, 50-51. Spelling and punctuation have been modernized.

II. Neither, secondly, would it invalidate our conclusion, that the watch sometimes went wrong, or that it seldom went exactly right. . . . It is not necessary that a machine be perfect in order to show with what design it was made: still less necessary, where the only question is whether it were made with any design at all.

III. Nor, thirdly, would it bring any uncertainty into the argument, if there were a few parts of the watch, concerning which we could not discover or had not yet discovered in what manner they conduced to the general effect; or even some parts, concerning which we could not ascertain whether they conduced to that effect in any manner whatever. . . . The indication of contrivance remained, with respect to them, nearly as it was before.

IV. Nor, fourthly, would any man in his senses think the existence of the watch with its various machinery accounted for, by being told that it was one out of possible combinations of material forms; that whatever he had found in the place where he found the watch, must have contained some internal configuration or other; and that this configuration might be the structure now exhibited, namely, of the works of a watch, as well as a different structure.

V. Nor, fifthly, would it yield his inquiry more satisfaction, to be answered that there existed in things a principle of order, which had disposed the parts of the watch into their present form and situation. He never knew a watch made by the principle of order; nor can he even form to himself an idea of what is meant by a principle of order distinct from the intelligence of the watchmaker.

VI. Sixthly, he would be surprised to hear that the mechanism of the watch was no proof of contrivance, only a motive to induce the mind to think so.

VII. And not less surprised to be informed that the watch in his hand was nothing more than the result of the laws of *metallic* nature. It is a perversion of language to assign any law as the efficient, operative cause of any thing. A law presupposes an agent, for it is only the mode according to which an agent proceeds: it implies a power, for it is the order according to which that power acts. Without this agent, without this power, which are both distinct from itself, the *law* does nothing, is nothing. . . .

VIII. Neither, lastly, would our observer be driven out of his conclusion, or from his confidence in its truth, by being told that he knew nothing at all about the matter. He knows enough for his argument; he knows the utility of the end; he knows the subserviency and adaptation of the means to the end. These points being known, his ignorance of other points, his doubts concerning other points, affect not the certainty of his reasoning. The consciousness of knowing little need not beget a distrust of that which he does know. . . .

Suppose, in the next place, that the person who found the watch should after some time discover that, in addition to all the properties which he had hitherto observed in it, it possessed the unexpected property of producing in the course of its movement another watch like itself . . . let us inquire what effect ought such a discovery to have upon his former conclusion.

I. The first effect would be to increase his admiration of the contrivance, and his conviction of the consummate skill of the contriver. . . .

II. He would reflect that, though the watch before him were in some sense the maker of the watch which was fabricated in the course of its movements, yet it was in a very different sense from that in which a carpenter, for instance, is the maker of a chair—the author of its contrivance, the cause of the relation of its parts to their use. With respect to these, the first watch was no cause at all to the second; in no such sense as this was it the author of the constitution and order, either of the parts which the new watch contained, or of the parts by the aid and instrumentality of which it was produced. . . .

III. Though it be now no longer probable that the individual watch which our observer had found was made immediately by the hand of an artificer, yet this alteration does not in anywise affect the inference that an artificer had been originally employed and concerned in the production. The argument from design remains as it was. . . . There cannot be design without a designer; contrivance without a contriver; order without choice; arrangement without anything capable of arranging; subserviency and relation to a purpose without that which could intend a purpose; means suitable to an end, and executing their office in accomplishing that end, without the end ever having been contemplated or the means accommodated to it. . . .

IV. Nor is anything gained by running the difficulty farther back, that is, by supposing the watch before us to have been produced from another watch that from a former, and so on indefinitely. . . . Contrivance is still unaccounted for. We still want a contriver. A designing mind is neither supposed by this supposition nor dispensed with. . . . Where there is a tendency, or, as we increase the number of terms, a continual approach toward a limit, there, by supposing the number of terms to be what is called infinite, we may conceive the limit to be attained; but where there is no such tendency or approach, nothing is effected by lengthening the series. . . . A chain composed of an infinite number of links can no more support itself than a chain composed of a finite number of links. . . .

Contrivance must have had a contriver, design a designer, whether the machine immediately proceeded from another machine or not. That circumstance alters not the case. . . .

V. Our observer would further also reflect that the maker of the watch before him was in truth and reality the maker of every watch produced from it: there being no difference, except that the latter manifests a more exquisite skill, ...

. . . What, as has already been said, but to increase beyond measure our admiration of the skill which had been employed in the formation of such a machine? Or shall it, instead of this, all at once turn us round to an opposite conclusion, namely, that no art or skill whatever has been concerned in the business, although all other evidences of art and skill remain as they were, and this last and supreme piece of art be now added to the rest? Can this be maintained without absurdity? . . .

Every observation which was made in our first chapter concerning the watch may be repeated with strict propriety concerning the eye, concerning animals, concerning plants, concerning, indeed, all the organized parts of the works of nature. As,

I. When we are inquiring simply after the *existence* of an intelligent Creator, imperfection, inaccuracy, liability to disorder, occasional irregularities may subsist in a considerable degree without inducing any doubt into the question. . . . Irregularities and imperfections are of little or no weight in the consideration when that consideration relates simply to the existence of a Creator. When the argument respects his attributes, they are of weight; but are then to be taken in conjunction—the attention is not to rest upon them, but they are to be taken in conjunction with the unexceptional evidences which we possess of skill, power, and benevolence displayed in other instances; which evidences may, in strength, number, and variety, be such and may so overpower apparent blemishes as to induce us, upon the most reasonable ground, to believe that these last ought to be referred to some cause, though we be ignorant of it, other than defect of knowledge or of benevolence in the author.

For Further Reading

LeMahieu, D. L. *The Mind of William Paley: A Philosopher and His Age.* Lincoln, Neb.: University of Nebraska Press, 1976.

Paley, William. *A View of the Evidences of Christianity.* New York: Harper, 1856.

———. *The Works of William Paley.* Philadelphia: Crissey and Markley, 1857.

11   Immanuel Kant

(1724–1804)

IMMANUEL KANT WAS BORN AND DIED IN THE SMALL
provincial East Prussian town of Königsberg. His parents' warmly
pietistic Christianity made a lasting impression on Kant and
influenced his thought throughout his professional career. Trained from
the beginning in philosophy, he pursued an academic career. He was
educated through the university level, leaving the university in 1746 to
work as a tutor for various families. In 1755 he took a master's degree at
the University of Königsberg and began teaching there as *Privatdozent*.
In 1770 he was appointed to the Chair of Logic and Metaphysics at
Königsberg.

In reading accounts of Kant's personal life, one gets the impression of a
philosopher totally devoted to his teaching and writing. He was the first
major philosopher of modern times to spend his life as a teacher of the
subject as well as a thinker. His passionate devotion to philosophy was
balanced by a singularly moderate lifestyle. His observable life was
altogether unremarkable. His single-minded devotion to philosophy
was at least in part responsible for his never marrying. In 1794, when the
Prussian king asked him not to publish any more on the topic of religion,
since his views upset people, Kant agreed not to do so, rather than stand
up against his king. He did what came his way to do, teaching and
writing and meeting his obligations as rector of the university. He was
fond of conversation with friends and with travelers who brought him
news of a world he never saw. Carefulness allowed him to remain in
good health, despite not being especially robust, nearly until the time of
his death at the age of eighty.[1]

Although considered a philosopher, Kant frequently dealt with theological topics; it can be said that he revolutionized theology. In his history of nineteenth-century Protestant theology, Claude Welch writes of Kant that he exercised greater influence over nineteenth-century theology than did any other thinker. Kant embodied the European Enlightenment's sure confidence in the powers of human reason. While he shared this Enlightenment principle, he was also keenly aware of the limits of reason, so that certainties were set in the context of firmly fixed boundaries. One of the boundaries of critical reason is that it is limited to the objects of experience. It cannot go beyond things-as-we-know-them to things-in-themselves. Thus, critical reason stops short of religious verities such as God and immortality.[2] The germinal nature of his theological thought cannot be ignored by anyone who seeks to understand the changes that came about in thinking about God after Kant.

Kant's major contribution to this enterprise is the development of his "critical philosophy" after 1770. The "critical" element in this philosophy has to do with his critique of the powers of human reason, his delineating a new set of limits on what the powers of reason could and could not do. In the *Critique of Pure Reason* (1781; second edition 1787), Kant dismantles the traditional arguments for God's existence. The categories relied upon in such arguments are correct and useful when applied to things in the sensible world. However, they cannot be applied to God, for whatever God is, God is *not* an object alongside other objects in the sensible world. The "bottom line," as it were, is that human reason which is finite, using finite categories, cannot reason its way to the infinite.

Kant demonstrates the problems involved in such reasoning by the idea of *antinomies*, pairs of metaphysical doctrines that contradict each other. He then develops what he regards as an irrefutable proof for each (irrefutable, that is, so long as one accepts the point of view assumed by the proponents of the proofs).

The fourth antinomy concerns God's existence: God exists; God does not exist. Kant believes there are only three legitimate ways of demonstrating God's existence: the ontological proof from the idea of God itself, the cosmological argument from the necessity of a first cause, and the argument from design. He then proceeds to destroy all three.

The destruction of the classical proofs does not, however, mean the end of belief in God. That there is no proof opens the way for belief, in fact. Kant's belief is not irrational or nonrational fideism but a rational justification of religious faith that has its basis in the human experience of the moral life. This justification is developed in *Critique of Practical Reason* (1790). There are two lines of thought here. We ought to strive for the highest good, which is perfection, or an infinite good. Being infinite, it would require infinite time and an immortal soul to even approach it. The moral experience thus calls for the idea of a God to underwrite the idea of immortality. In the second place, the moral agent feels called upon to bring about a situation in which happiness and virtue are proportionate to one another, to achieve the supreme good (summum bonum). However, experience tells us that we cannot do this in this world unaided by anything beyond ourselves. Thus, if such an agent takes the moral course of making a commitment to action toward this end, such action demonstrates belief in a moral author of the universe who wills and can bring about the desired end.

Morality must be based on duty alone. It will not do to have it based on divine command nor on either the promise of divine reward or the threat of divine punishment. Kant is absolutely clear on this point. Morality is thus not based upon God. The idea of the being of God is based upon the experience of the moral life.

* * *

MORALITY NEEDS GOD

Critique of All Theology Based upon Speculative Principles of Reason

If by the term *Theology* I understand the cognition of a primal being, that cognition is based either upon reason alone (*theologia rationalis*) or upon revelation (*theologia revelata*). The former cogitates its object either by means of pure transcendental conceptions, as an *ends originarium, realissimum, ends entium*, and is termed *transcendental theology*; or, by means of a conception derived from the nature of our own mind, as a supreme intelligence, and must then be entitled *natural theology*. . . .

Transcendental theology aims either at inferring the existence of a Supreme Being from a general experience—without any closer reference to the world to which this experience belongs, and in this case it is called *Cosmotheology*; or it endeavors to cognize the existence of such a being,

---

The first selection, beginning on p. 116, is from Immanuel Kant, *Critique of Pure Reason*, trans. J. M. D. Meiklejohn (New York: P. F. Collier & Son, 1901), pp. 353-57.

The second selection, beginning on p. 118, is from Immanuel Kant, *Critique of Practical Reason*, trans. Thomas Kingsmill Abbott (London: Longmans, Green and Co., Ltd., 1909), pp. 218-22, 229-31.

through mere conceptions, without the aid of experience, and is then termed *Ontotheology*.

Natural theology infers the attributes and the existence of an author of the world, from the constitution of, the order and unity observable in, the world, in which two modes of causality must be admitted to exist—those of nature and freedom. Thus it rises from this world to a supreme intelligence, either as the principle of all natural, or of all moral order and perfection. . . .

. . . We shall at some future time show that the moral laws not merely presuppose the existence of a Supreme Being, but also, as themselves absolutely necessary in a different relation, demand or postulate it—although only from a practical point of view. The discussion of this argument we postpone for the present.

When the question relates merely to that which is, not to that which ought to be, the conditioned which is presented in experience, is always cogitated as contingent. For this reason its condition cannot be regarded as absolutely necessary, but merely as relatively necessary, or rather as *needful*. . . .

Now I maintain that all attempts of reason to establish a theology by the aid of speculation alone are fruitless, that the principles of reason as applied to nature do not conduct us to any theological truths, and, consequently, that a rational theology can have no existence, unless it is founded upon the laws of morality. For all synthetical principles of the understanding are valid only as *immanent* in experience; while the cognition of a Supreme Being necessitates their being employed transcendentally, and of this the understanding is quite incapable. If the empirical law of causality is to conduct us to a Supreme Being, this being must belong to the chain of empirical objects—in which case it would be, like all phenomena, itself conditioned. If the possibility of passing the limits of experience be admitted, by means of the dynamical law of the relation of an effect to its cause, what kind of conception shall we obtain by this procedure? Certainly not the conception of a Supreme Being, because experience never presents us with the greatest of all possible effects, and it is only an effect of this character that could witness to the existence of a corresponding cause. If, for the purpose of fully satisfying the requirements of Reason, we recognize her right to assert the existence of a perfect and absolutely necessary being, this can be admitted only from favor, and cannot be regarded as the result of irresistible demonstration. The psysico-theological proof may add weight to others—if other proofs there are—by connecting speculation with experience; but in itself it rather prepares the mind for theological cognition, and gives it a right and natural direction, than establishes a sure foundation for theology.

It is now perfectly evident that transcendental questions admit only of transcendental answers—those presented *à priori* by pure conceptions without the least empirical admixture. But the question in the present case is evidently synthetical—it aims at the extension of our cognition beyond the bounds of experience—it requires an assurance respecting the existence of a being corresponding with the idea in our minds, to which no experience can ever be adequate. Now it has been abundantly proved that all *à priori* synthetical cognition is possible only as the expression of the formal conditions of a possible experience; and that the validity of all principles depends upon their immanence in the field of experience, that is, their relation to objects of empirical cognition, or phenomena. Thus all transcendental procedure in reference to speculative theology is without result.

The Immortality of the Soul as a Postulate of Pure Practical Reason

The realization of the *summum bonum* in the world is the necessary object of a will determinable by the moral law. But in this will the *perfect accordance* of the mind with the moral law is the supreme condition of the *summum bonum*. This then must be possible, as well as its object, since it is contained in the command to promote the latter. Now, the perfect accordance of the will with the moral law is *holiness*, a perfection of which no rational being of the sensible world is capable at any moment of his existence. Since, nevertheless, it is required as practically necessary, it can only be found in a *progress in infinitum* towards that perfect accordance, and on the principles of pure practical reason it is necessary . . . to assume such a practical progress as the real object of our will.

Now, this endless progress is only possible on the supposition of an *endless* duration of the *existence* and personality of the same rational being (which is called the immortality of the soul). The *summum bonum*, then, practically is only possible on the supposition of the immortality of the soul; consequently this immortality, being inseparably connected with the moral law, is a postulate of pure practical reason (by which I mean a *theoretical* proposition, not demonstrable as such, but which is an inseparable result of an unconditional *à priori practical law*).

This principle of the moral destination of our nature, namely, that it is only in an endless progress that we can attain perfect accordance with the moral law, is of the greatest use, not merely for the present purpose of supplementing the impotence of speculative reason, but also with respect to religion. In default of it, either the moral law is quite degraded from its *holiness*, being made out to be *indulgent*, and conformable to our convenience, or else men strain their notions of their vocation and their expectation to an unattainable goal, hoping to acquire complete holiness of will, and so they lose themselves in fantastical *theosophic* dreams, which wholly contradict self-knowledge. In both cases the unceasing *effort* to obey punctually and thoroughly a strict and inflexible command of reason, which yet is not ideal but real, is only hindered. For a rational but finite being, the only thing possible is an endless progress from the lower to higher degrees of moral perfection. The *Infinite* Being, to whom the condition of time is nothing, . . . sees in this to us endless succession a whole of accordance with the moral law; and the holiness which His command inexorably requires, in order to be true to His justice in the share which He assigns to each in the *summum bonum*, is to be found in a single intellectual intuition of the whole existence of rational beings. All that can be expected of the creature in respect of the hope of this participation would be the consciousness of his tried character, by which, from the progress he has hitherto made from the worse to the morally better, and the immutability of purpose which has thus become known to him, he may hope for a further unbroken continuance of the same, however long his existence may last, even beyond this life, and thus he may hope, not indeed here, nor in any imaginable point of his future existence, but only in the endlessness of his duration (which God alone can survey) . . . to be perfectly adequate to his will (without indulgence or excuse, which do not harmonize with justice). . . .

In the foregoing analysis the moral law led to a practical problem which is prescribed by pure reason alone, without the aid of any sensible motives, namely, that of the necessary completeness of the first and principal element of the *summum bonum*, viz. Morality; and as this can be perfectly solved only in eternity, to the postulate of *immortality*. The same law must also lead us to affirm the possibility of the second element of the *summum bonum*, viz. Happiness proportioned to that morality, and this on grounds as disinterested as before, and solely from impartial reason; that is, it must lead to the supposition of the existence of a cause adequate to this effect; in other words, it must postulate the *existence of God*, as the necessary condition of the possibility of the *summum bonum* (an object of the will which is necessarily connected with the moral legislation of pure reason). We proceed to exhibit this connexion in a convincing manner.

Happiness is the condition of a rational being in the world with whom *everything goes according to his wish and will;* it rests, therefore, on the harmony of physical nature with his whole end, and likewise with the essential determining principle of his will. Now the moral law as a law of freedom commands by determining principles, . . . which ought to be quite independent on nature and on its harmony with our faculty of desire (as springs). But the acting rational being in the world is not the cause of the world and of nature itself. There is not the least ground, therefore, in the moral law for a necessary connexion between morality and proportionate happiness in a being that belongs to the world as part of it, and therefore dependent on it, and which for that reason cannot by his will be a cause of this nature, nor by his own power make it thoroughly harmonize, as far as his happiness is concerned, with his practical principles. Nevertheless, in the practical problem of pure reason, *i.e.* the necessary pursuit of the *summum bonum,* such a connexion is postulated as necessary: we ought to endeavour to promote the *summum bonum,* which, therefore, must be possible. Accordingly, the existence of a cause of all nature, distinct from nature itself, and containing the principle of this connexion, namely, of the exact harmony of happiness with morality, is also *postulated.* Now, this supreme cause must contain the principle of the harmony of nature, not merely with a law of the will of rational beings, but with the conception of this *law,* in so far as they make it the *supreme determining principle of the will,* and consequently not merely with the form of morals, but with their morality as their motive, that is, with their moral character. Therefore, the *summum bonum* is possible in the world only on the supposition of a Supreme Being having a causality corresponding to moral character. Now a being that is capable of acting on the conception of laws is an *intelligence* (a rational being), and the causality of such a being according to this conception of laws is his *will;* therefore the supreme cause of nature, which must be presupposed as a condition of the *summum bonum* . . . is a being which is the cause of nature by *intelligence* and *will,* consequently its author, that is God. It follows that the postulate of the possibility of the *highest derived good* (the best world) is likewise the postulate of the reality of a *highest original good,* that is to say, of the existence of God. Now it was seen to be a duty for us to promote the *summum bonum;* consequently it is not merely allowable, but it is a necessity connected with duty as a requisite, that we should presuppose the possibility of this *summum bonum;* and as this is possible only on condition of the existence of God, it inseparably connects the supposition of this with duty; that is, it is morally necessary to assume the existence of God. . . .

They all proceed from the principle of morality, which is not a postulate but a law, by which reason determines the will directly, which will, because it is so determined as a pure will, requires these necessary conditions of obedience to its precept. These postulates are not theoretical dogmas but, suppositions practically necessary; while then they do [not] extent our speculative knowledge, they give`objective reality to the ideas of speculative reason in general (by means of their reference to what is practical), and give it a right to concepts, the possibility even of which it could not otherwise venture to affirm.

These postulates are those *of immortality, freedom* positively considered (as the causality of a being so far as he belongs to the intelligible world), and the *existence of God.* The *first* results from the practically necessary condition of a duration . . . adequate to the complete fulfilment of the moral law; the *second* from the necessary supposition of independence on the sensible world, and of the faculty of determining one's will according to the law of an intelligible world, that is, of freedom; the *third* from the necessary condition of the existence of the *summum bonum* in such an intelligible world, by the supposition of the supreme independent good, that is, the existence of God.

Thus the fact that respect for the moral law necessarily makes the *summum bonum* an object of our endeavours, and the supposition thence resulting of its objective reality, lead through the postulates of practical reason to conceptions which speculative reason might indeed present as problems, but could never solve. Thus it leads—1. To that one in the solution of which the latter could do nothing but commit *paralogisms* (namely, that of immortality), because it could not lay hold of the character of permanence, by which to complete the psychological conception of an ultimate subject necessarily ascribed to the soul in self-consciousness, so as to make it the real conception of a substance, a character which practical reason furnishes by the postulate of a duration required for accordance with the moral law in the *summum bonum,* which is the whole end of practical reason. 2. It leads to that of which speculative reason contained nothing but *antinomy,* the solution of which it could only found on a notion problematically conceivable indeed, but whose objective reality it could not prove or determine, namely, the *cosmological* idea of an intelligible world and the consciousness of our existence in it, by means of the postulate of freedom (the reality of which it lays down by virtue of the moral law), and with it likewise the law of an intelligible world, to which speculative reason could only point, but could not define its conception. 3. What speculative reason was able to think, but was obliged to leave undetermined as a mere transcendental *ideal,* . . . viz. the *theological* conception of the First Being, to this it gives significance (in a practical view, that is, as a condition of the possibility of the object of a will determined by that law), namely, as the supreme principle of the *summum bonum* in an intelligible world, by means of moral legislation in it invested with sovereign power.

Is our knowledge, however, actually extended in this way by pure practical reason, and is that *immanent* in practical reason which for the speculative was only *transcendent*? Certainly, but *only in a practical point of view*. For we do not thereby take knowledge of the nature of our souls, nor of the intelligible world, nor of the Supreme Being, with respect to what they are in themselves, but we have merely combined the conceptions of them in the *practical* concept of the *summum bonum* as the object of our will, and this altogether *à priori*, but only by means of the moral law, and merely in reference to it, in respect of the object which it commands. But how freedom is possible, and how we are to conceive this kind of causality theoretically and positively, is not thereby discovered; but only that there is such a causality is postulated by the moral law and in its behoof. It is the same with the remaining ideas, the possibility of which no human intelligence will ever fathom, but the truth of which, on the other hand, no sophistry will ever wrest from the conviction even of the commonest man.

For Further Reading

Cassirer, Ernst. *Kant's Life and Thought*. Trans. James Haden. New Haven, Conn.: Yale University Press, 1981.

Kant, Immanuel. *Religion Within the Limits of Reason Alone*. Trans. Theodore M. Greene and Hoyt H. Hudson. New York: Harper & Row, 1960.

THE
DICHOTOMY
TRANSCENDED

Paul Tillich

(1886–1965)

PAUL TILLICH WAS BORN IN THE PARISH HOUSE IN THE small German community of Starzeddel near Berlin, where his father Johannes was a Lutheran pastor. One biographer characterized the young Tillich as a "serious and somewhat spoiled" child.[1] He studied at the Humanistic Gymnasium at Königsberg and at the Friedrich Wilhelm Gymnasium in Berlin. In 1910 he received the Doctorate in Philosophy at Breslau and two years later received the Licentiate of Theology at the University of Halle and was ordained a pastor in the Evangelical Church of the Prussian Union.

From 1914 to 1918 the young pastor served as an Army chaplain on the Western front, an encounter with hostility, death, and courage that would leave a permanent impression on his work. He then turned to teaching from 1919 to 1933, holding various posts in philosophy, religion, and theology at Berlin, Marburg, Dresden, Leipzig, and Frankfurt am Main. Like his contemporary and fellow educator Karl Barth, Tillich was dismissed from his teaching post in 1933 by the Hitler regime. Almost immediately Tillich emigrated to the United States. His teaching career there spanned the years 1933 to 1965 and reads like a "Where's Where" of liberal Protestant educational institutions: Columbia University, Union Theological Seminary (New York), Harvard, and the Divinity School at the University of Chicago.

Tillich died in the fall of 1965 and was interred in Tillich Park at New Harmony, Indiana, in the spring of 1966, three years after the park was dedicated to his life and work.

Tillich's theological thinking took place on the boundary between his

124

interpretation of Christian faith and the secular world—its culture, art and literature, the sciences and the humanities. For Tillich, there is nothing that in principle cannot be religious. Religion points to the depth dimension of everything, rather than being a separate realm. Religion is "ultimate concern," whatever the specific content of that concern may be for a given individual. This viewpoint permitted Tillich to speak to people who were alienated from traditional religion, those for whom the ideas and symbols of Christianity had lost their power. This is illustrated clearly in this passage from a sermon entitled "The Depth of Existence." In this passage, Tillich advises that if the word "God" does not have meaning for an individual, it can be translated into other terms. It is the depths of one's life, the source of one's being, and that which is taken with utmost seriousness, without reservation. It is permissible and may even be necessary to forget all of what one has learned of God, and to cease using the word itself, overladen with traditional meanings, in order to recover its vital, living meaning for oneself. In plumbing one's own greatest depths fully, one will find, if not God, then the meaning of God.[2]

Tillich's theology, influenced as it was by existentialism and depth psychology, displays a breadth and a depth that have few equals. There is an emotional involvement that vibrates through even his most abstract theology. It is most evident in the sermons, which are at the same time highly intellectual, but it can be heard also even in the most philosophical parts of the Systematic Theology. Commentators have likened Tillich to earlier theologians of the caliber of Augustine, Aquinas, Calvin, and Schleiermacher. Although the Protestant principle of continual self-criticism in theology does not ever allow there to be a final and complete theology, theologians of great stature succeed in uniting the best of secular thought in a particular era with God's revelation. Tillich was such a theologian.[3]

Tillich's determination to keep theology in constant dialogue with the rest of human life and culture takes specific shape in his "method of correlation," his distinctive contribution to the discussion of faith and reason, or the divine and the human in the formation of ideas about God. He explains this method in his Systematic Theology. Whether consciously and overtly or less consciously, theologians have always done theology in dialogue with their culture, simply because people are always products of their socio-cultural setting, to an extent.

The method of correlation brings together "existential questions" and "theological answers" in a true dialogue. It must do so if theology is to speak to culture. The "existential questions" are those perennial, burning human questions that arise out of the depth of our humanity; we *are* the question, prior to asking any specific questions. Understanding and expressing the human question for a given culture is aided by many disciplines—philosophy, literature, the arts, psychology, and sociology, among others. This analysis, even when done by a theologian, is a philosophical one.

Formulating the answers is the proper task of theology. In light of what is perceived as God's revelation, the theologian frames the theological answers to human questions in response to the questions themselves. The way the questions are formulated in and for a given culture does influence the answers that are given. There is no single answer for all times and places. Questions and answers stand together in "mutual interdependence." The dialogue, when pursued unflaggingly, leads to a point at which question and answer are not separate but fused together into a new reality.[4]

The method of correlation is reflected clearly in the structure of Tillich's Systematic Theology. Each section and each discussion of a doctrine begins by an analysis of the existential question or questions to which the doctrine provides an answer. That answer is then cast in terms that themselves arise out of how the questions were asked. We see here a method of doing theology which is the opposite of Barth's emphasis on the absolute priority of the answers.

Tillich uses the method of correlation as a replacement for at least three views that he considers inadequate. It replaces the propositional view of revelation in which revelation is understood as the giving of supernatural information. It replaces "humanistic" liberal theology, which tends to derive its answers from human existence, not taking sufficient account of human brokenness and sin. And finally, it replaces natural theology and the "arguments" for God's existence.[5]

The reading selection, in which Tillich's controversial idea of the "God beyond the God of theism" is presented, shows the method of correlation at work as a way of transcending the standard theological dichotomies of faith versus reason, revelation versus discovery.

* * *

THE GOD BEYOND GOD

Courage is the self-affirmation of being in spite of the fact of nonbeing. It is the act of the individual self in taking the anxiety of nonbeing upon

From Paul Tillich, The Courage To Be (New Haven, Conn.: Yale University Press, 1952), pp. 155-56, 172, 178-81, 182-86, 187-89. Copyright © 1952 by Yale University Press. Reprinted by permission of publisher.

itself by affirming itself either as part of an embracing whole or in its individual selfhood. Courage always includes a risk, it is always threatened by nonbeing, whether the risk of losing oneself and becoming a thing within the whole of things or of losing one's world in an empty self-relatedness. Courage needs the power of being, a power transcending the nonbeing which is experienced in the anxiety of fate and death, which is present in the anxiety of emptiness and meaninglessness, which is effective in the anxiety of guilt and condemnation. The courage which takes this threefold anxiety into itself must be rooted in a power of being that is greater than the power of oneself and the power of one's world. . . . There are no exceptions to this rule; and this means that every courage to be has an open or hidden religious root. For religion is the state of being grasped by the power of being-itself. . . .

. . . Faith is the state of being grasped by the power of being-itself. The courage to be is an expression of faith and what "faith" means must be understood through the courage to be. We have defined courage as the self-affirmation of being in spite of nonbeing. The power of this self-affirmation is the power of being which is effective in every act of courage. Faith is the experience of this power. . . .

The courage to be in all its forms has, by itself, revelatory character. It shows the nature of being, it shows that the self-affirmation of being is an affirmation that overcomes negation. In a metaphorical statement (and every assertion about being-itself is either metaphorical or symbolic) one could say that being includes nonbeing but nonbeing does not prevail against it. "Including" is a spatial metaphor which indicates that being embraces itself and that which is opposed to it, nonbeing. Nonbeing belongs to being, it cannot be separated from it. . . .

But where there is nonbeing there is finitude and anxiety. If we say that nonbeing belongs to being-itself, we say that finitude and anxiety belong to being-itself. Wherever philosophers or theologians have spoken of the divine blessedness they have implicitly (and sometimes explicitly) spoken of the anxiety of finitude which is eternally taken into the blessedness of the divine infinity. The infinite embraces itself and the finite, the Yes includes itself and the No which it takes into itself, blessedness comprises itself and the anxiety of which it is the conquest. All this is implied if one says that being includes nonbeing and that through nonbeing it reveals itself. It is a highly symbolic language which must be used at this point. But its symbolic character does not diminish its truth; on the contrary, it is a condition of its truth. To speak unsymbolically about being-itself is untrue.

The divine self-affirmation is the power that makes the self-affirmation of the finite being, the courage to be, possible. Only because being-itself has the character of self-affirmation in spite of nonbeing is courage possible. Courage participates in the self-affirmation of being-itself, it participates in the power of being which prevails against nonbeing. He who receives this power in an act of mystical or personal or absolute faith is aware of the source of his courage to be.

. . . Not arguments but the courage to be reveals the true nature of being-itself. By affirming our being we participate in the self-affirmation of being-itself. There are no valid arguments for the "existence" of God, but there are acts of courage in which we affirm the power of being, whether we know it or not. . . . Courage has revealing power, the courage to be is the key to being-itself.

The courage to take meaninglessness into itself presupposes a relation to the ground of being which we have called "absolute faith." It is without a *special* content, yet it is not without content. The content of absolute faith is the "God above God." Absolute faith and its consequence, the courage that takes the radical doubt, the doubt about God, into itself, transcends the theistic idea of God.

Theism can mean the unspecified affirmation of God. Theism in this sense does not say what it means if it uses the name of God. . . .

Theism can have another meaning, quiet contrary to the first one: it can be the name of what we have called the divine-human encounter. In this case it points to those elements in the Jewish-Christian tradition which emphasize the person-to-person relationship with God. . . .

Theism has a third meaning, a strictly theological one. Theological theism is, like every theology, dependent on the religious substance which it conceptualizes. It is dependent on theism in the first sense insofar as it tries to prove the necessity of affirming God in some way; it usually develops the so-called arguments for the "existence" of God. . . .

Now theism in the first sense must be transcended because it is irrelevant, and theism in the second sense must be transcended because it is one-sided. But theism in the third sense must be transcended because it is wrong. It is bad theology. This can be shown by a more penetrating analysis. The God of theological theism is a being beside others and as such a part of the whole of reality. . . . He is a being, not being-itself. As such he is bound to the subject-object structure of reality, he is an object for us as subjects. At the same time we are objects for him as a subject. And this is decisive for the necessity of transcending theological theism. For God as a subject makes me into an object which is nothing more than an object. He deprives me of my subjectivity because he is all-powerful and all knowing. . . .

Theism in all its forms is transcended in the experience we have called absolute faith. It is the accepting of the acceptance without somebody or something that accepts. It is the power of being-itself that accepts and gives the courage to be. . . .

The ultimate source of the courage to be is the "God above God"; this is the result of our demand to transcend theism. Only if the God of theism is transcended can the anxiety of doubt and meaninglessness be taken into the courage to be. . . .

. . . The acceptance of the God above the God of theism makes us a part of that which is not also a part but is the ground of the whole. . . .

Absolute faith, or the state of being grasped by the God beyond God, is not a state which appears beside other states of the mind. It never is something separated and definite, an event which could be isolated and described. It is always a movement in, with, and under other states of the mind. It is the situation on the boundary of man's possibilities. It is this boundary. Therefore it is both the courage of despair and the courage in and above every courage. It is not a place where one can live, it is without the safety of words and concepts, it is without a name, a church, a cult, a theology. But it is moving in the depth of all of them. It is the power of being, in which they participate and of which they are fragmentary expressions. . . .

. . . The courage to take the anxiety of meaninglessness upon oneself is the boundary line up to which the courage to be can go. Beyond it is mere non-being. Within it all forms of courage are re-established in the power of the God above the God of theism. *The courage to be is rooted in the God who appears when God has disappeared in the anxiety of doubt.*

For Further Reading

Adams, James Luther. *Paul Tillich's Philosophy of Culture, Science and Religion.* New York: Schocken Books, 1965.

Kegley, Charles W., and Robert W. Bretall. *The Theology of Paul Tillich.* New York: Macmillan, 1964.

Pauck, Wilhelm, and Marion Pauck. *Paul Tillich: His Life and Thought.* Vol. 1, *Life.* New York: Harper & Row, 1976.

Tillich, Paul. *Dynamics of Faith.* New York: Harper & Row, 1957.

_____. *The Eternal Now.* New York: Charles Scribner's Sons, 1963.

_____. *The New Being.* New York: Charles Scribner's Sons, 1955.

_____. *The Shaking of the Foundations.* New York: Charles Scribner's Sons, 1948.

_____. *Systematic Theology.* 3 vols. Chicago: University of Chicago Press, 1967.

Julian Huxley

(1887–1975)

JULIAN HUXLEY WAS BUT ONE MEMBER OF A DISTINGUISHED British family including authors Leonard Huxley, Thomas Henry Huxley, and Aldous Huxley. Far from being overshadowed by his well-known relatives, Julian Huxley made his own reputation as a biologist, writer, and philosopher. In 1946 he was elected director general of UNESCO (United Nations Educational, Scientific, and Cultural Organization), a post in which he made valuable contributions to developing the organization's basic philosophy.

Huxley's approach to religion is a naturalistic one. That is to say, he rejects all explanations of religion in supernatural, other-worldly terms, in favor of an explanation that remains firmly anchored in this world. This does not, however, lead Huxley to reject religion as such. For Julian Huxley, religion arises as the profoundly human response to (1) our very human concern for our destiny and role in the world and, perhaps more basically, (2) the sacred dimension people perceive in the world itself. This latter is clearly akin to the experience of the Holy about which Rudolf Otto writes in The Idea of the Holy and to Friedrich Schleiermacher's "sense and taste for the Infinite"[1] (without, however, being linked to the presupposition of the existence of an infinite, supernatural Being).

Huxley's world is best characterized as an infinitely extending creative process, guided always by principles immanent in the process itself. Human beings are the primary agents of this creativity, since people have the unique capacity to reflect upon the process and attempt to alter it instead of merely being swept along with it. From this unique human vantage point, questions of destiny and the experience of sacredness arise.

Huxley's *Religion Without Revelation* stands as his most thorough-going attempt to present a wholly naturalistic theory of the origin and development of religion. His general approach, as well as his keen humanistic concern for the fate of the world and humankind, are summarized in the book's preface. It is erroneous to suppose that religion cannot be scientifically analyzed simply because religious experience differs from scientific experience. It is a phenomenon like any other. The use of scientific methods has steadily expanded into new fields, and lately into the field of religion. Such disciplines as comparative religion and the psychology of religion have advanced our understanding of religion already.

According to Huxley, one of the results of such investigation is the dawning awareness that "God" is not the only hypothesis that accounts for human destiny, and that furthermore, it may well prove to be an inadequate one. He calls for a monistic rather than a dualistic view, a way that unites old and new, subject and object, science and spirituality. To develop such a system is an urgent task for humankind as a whole.[2]

* * *

THE NATURALISTIC IMPERATIVE

There are, it seems to me, three possible ways of envisaging and defining the nature of gods. In briefest terms, the first is that gods have real independent existence as personal but supernatural beings able to control or influence the natural world. The second is that gods are personalized representations, created by human minds, of the forces affecting human destiny. And the third, which is in a sense a compromise between the other two, is that they are more or less adequate attempts by man to describe or denote a single eternal suprapersonal and supernatural Being with a real existence behind or above nature. . . .

. . . In the light of our present knowledge I maintain that only the second is tenable—that gods are creations of man, personalized representations of the forces of destiny, with their unity projected into them by human thought and imagination.

In parentheses I should say that I do *not* mean only our present knowledge in the field of natural science, but also our knowledge in the

From Julian Huxley, *Religion Without Revelation* (New York: Harper & Bros., 1957). Selections are arranged in the following order: from chap. 3, pp. 47-50; from chap. 1, pp. 1-22; from chap. 5, pp. 110-23. Reprinted by permission of A. D. Peters & Co., Ltd.

fields of history, prehistory, and cultural anthropology, of human psychology and of comparative religion.

This general statement on the nature of gods can be profitably reformulated and spelled out somewhat as follows. History shows an increasingly successful extension of the naturalistic approach to more and more fields of experience, coupled with a progressive failure and restriction of supernaturalist interpretation. The time has now come for a naturalistic approach to theology. In the light of this approach, gods appear as interpretative concepts or hypotheses. They are hypotheses aiming at fuller comprehension of the facts of human destiny, in the same way that scientific hypotheses aim at fuller comprehension of the facts of nature. They are theoretical constructions of the human mind, in the same way as are scientific theories and concepts: and, like scientific theories and laws, they are based on experience and observable facts. . . .

I have called this book *Religion without Revelation* in order to express at the outset my conviction that religion of the highest and fullest character can co-exist with a complete absence of belief in revelation in any straightforward sense of the word, and of belief in that kernel of revealed religion, a personal god. . . .

. . . In the first place, I believe, not that there *is* nothing, for that I do not know, but that we quite assuredly at present *know* nothing beyond this world and natural experience. A personal God, be he Jehovah, or Allah, or Apollo, or Amen-Ra, or without name but simply God, I *know* nothing of. What is more, I am not merely agnostic on the subject. It seems to me quite clear that the idea of personality in God or in any supernatural being or beings has been put there by man, put into and round a perfectly real conception which we might continue to call God if the word had not acquired by long association the implication of a personal being; and therefore I disbelieve in a personal God in any sense in which that phrase is ordinarily used.

For similar reasons, I disbelieve in the existence of Heaven or Hell in any conventional Christian sense. . . .

As to the existence of another world or another life at all, there I am simply agnostic: I do not know. I find extreme difficulties, in the light of physiological and psychological knowledge, in understanding how a soul could exist apart from a body; but difficulties are never disproof. . . .

What, then, is religion? It is a way of life. It is a way of life which follows necessarily from a man's holding certain things in reverence, from his feeling and believing them to be sacred. And those things which are held sacred by religion primarily concern human destiny and the forces with which it comes into contact.

. . . I wish to emphasize at the outset that I am speaking in the most general terms, and that this specifically religious emotion of sacredness may be felt in relation to any object or thought, within or without the bounds of what we may be accustomed to think of as religion, within or without the bounds of any organized religious system.

The idea of supernatural beings is one of the commonest among the objects, events, or ideas which are thus believed in as objects of reverence; but belief in supernatural beings is not an essential or integral part of the religious way of life, nor, conversely, are the objects of religious feeling necessarily supernatural beings.

I believe, then, that religion arose as a feeling of the sacred. The capacity for experiencing this feeling in relation to various objects and events seems to be a fundamental capacity of man, something given in and by the construction of the normal human mind, just as definitely as is the capacity for experiencing anger or admiration, sympathy or terror. What is more, we experience each of these feelings or sentiments in relation to certain general kinds of situations. There is no specific connection between any given object and a particular feeling, but there does exist one type of situation in which men tend to feel anger, another in which they tend to feel admiration, another in which they tend to feel reverence. But (and a very important *but*) in every case, the type of situation which tends to arouse any particular feeling is always found to alter with experience and education. Many of the situations which arouse fear in a child cease to arouse fear when he has grown up; many situations which arouse fear in a young savage would not do so in a civilized child of the same age; and vice versa.

So it is with the religious feeling, the sentiment of sacredness. No one expects a child of four to have the same kind of religious life as a boy of sixteen, or either of them as a man of thirty. Nor should any one expect a savage to have arrived at the same religious attitude as a civilized man with different cultural background and with centuries of developing tradition at his back. The situations which arouse the religious feeling cannot be expected to be the same in the various cases. This elementary truth has, however, not been grasped by many missionaries and missionary societies; and the failure to grasp it has often led to disastrous results.

The history of religion is the history of the gradual change in the situations which, with increase of experience and changed conditions of life, are felt as sacred. . . .

This change is effected in a number of ways. In the first place, man reasons about his religious feelings and thoughts, or at least attempts to find reasons by which they may be justified. By this means, in relation to a mainly emotional, non-rational ground or raw material of religion, an intellectual scheme is brought into being, a definite set of beliefs, a primitive theology. The beliefs and their objects are intimately associated with the original pervading sense of sacredness, and so themselves come to be felt as sacred. The precise details of the process, in so far as it can be pieced together from history and from the study of comparative religion, are complex; I shall try to explore them a little more fully in a later chapter. The main and most essential steps appear to have been, first, the personification of the powers revered and religiously feared as brooding over human destiny; then the progressive unification of these powers, resulting in the substitution of few gods for innumerable spirits; and finally the fading or fusing of the several gods into one God.

Meanwhile an analogous process had been taking place on the moral side. With increase of physical control and intellectual comprehension, human destiny was seen to be more and more a matter of morality; the acquisition of the sense of personal holiness, less a matter of ritual or propitiation, more a matter of righteousness. Inevitably, in such circumstances, the governance of the world came to appear more concerned with morality, less a mere affair of arbitrary power. And since the idea of supernatural beings was by this time firmly enthroned as part and parcel of religion, moral qualities were increasingly ascribed to spirits and to gods. . . .

. . . [Just] as the logical intellect and the thirst for ever more ultimate causes pushed on the unification of the separate personal gods, and demonstrated them, against the inertia of tradition and so-called common sense, to be but different aspects of a single more ultimate divinity, so the logic of the moral sense and the craving to make out of a disconnected series of acts, moral in different ways and degrees, an organized moral life with all its parts related, led to unification in the moral sphere as well. Moral contradictions were gradually eliminated from the character of god, and different aspects of that character came to be more highly exalted—love, for instance, being elevated into the supreme place, above power and above justice.

A very similar process runs its course in the growing mind of every individual human being who does not merely put on a reach-me-down religion, but with intellectual and moral effort, often with pain and grief, achieves his own religious development. His ideas are at first little more than states of feeling, experienced perhaps deeply but with vagueness and without comprehension. His reason develops, and he cannot help but try to use it to make sense of the sacred chaos. His moral sense grows, he becomes the prey of moral conflicts: if he is to attain to peace of mind and stable maturity, he must adjust the warring interests, and see that order and unity are masters in his moral house. He must, too, bring his moral and his intellectual schemes into some reasonable relation with each other, and both into relation with his feeling of what is worthy to be held sacred.

The essential of all this, to my mind, is that religion is an activity of man which suffers change like all other human activities; that it may change for the better or for the worse; that if it stand still and refuse to change when other human activities are changing, then the standing still is itself a change for the worse; that as it grows, it cannot avoid coming into contact both with intellectual and with moral or ethical problems; and that with the development and broadening of human experience and tradition, religion becomes inevitably preoccupied with the intellectual comprehension of man's relation to the universe, and with the attainment of a coherent and unified moral life as well as with its more original quest for emotional satisfaction in the sphere of the holy. . . . Finally, in its most developed and highest manifestations, this emotional side of the religious life aspires to a sense of communion with the divine, and to the peace and security which spring from the surrender of the individual will to what is usually described as the will of God.

It remains now, very briefly, for me to make some preliminary statement as to how I would interpret the religious view of God, since this, and all its corollaries, seems to me to be the one essential point of different outstanding between 'religion' and 'science' to-day—religion in the sense not only of Christian orthodoxy but of all theism, and science not only in the sense of physics, chemistry, or biology, but of organized knowledge and thought based upon a naturalistic outlook.

Once adjust this difficulty, and there remains no conflict of principle. All the vital facts of religious life still remain: they but want re-defining in new terms. The living reality will need to change its clothes—that is all. . . .

On this view man's idea of the divine, and his expression of it, is on a par with his discovery and formulation of intellectual truth, his apprehension and expression of beauty, his perception and his practice of moral laws. There is no revelation concerned in it more than the revelation concerned in scientific discovery, no different kind of inspiration in the Bible from that in Shelley's poetry. . . .

If we were prepared to admit that the ascription of personality or external spiritual nature to gods were an illusion or an error, our comparison of religion with science or with art would then be complete. Each then would be a fusion of external fact with inner capacity into vital experience (or, looked at from a slightly different angle, each is an expression of that vital experience). There does exist an outer ground and object of religion as much as an outer object of science. The fact, however, that this outer object is by most religions considered to be an external divine being is, philosophically speaking, an accident; it remains real whether so considered or not, just as the outer objects of science remain real whether we consider that laws of nature inhere in them or in the human mind. Not only so, but the ascription of personal being to religion's external object is best thought of as in origin a natural and inevitable error of primitive thinking, now surviving in highly modified form, a mistaken projection of personality into the non-personal. It is thus an error of judgment comparable (though on a larger scale) to the alchemist's error in superposing on the facts of chemistry, as then known, his belief in transmutation and the philosopher's stone, or the error of early biology in superposing on the facts of putrefaction a belief in spontaneous generation.

If, however, this superposed belief and its corollaries be removed, what remains of the reality? The answer is 'a great deal.' That reality includes permanent facts of human existence—birth, marriage, reproduction, and death; suffering, mutual aid, comradeship, physical and moral growth. It includes also other facts which we may call the facts of the spiritual life, such as the conviction of sin, the desire for righteousness, the sense of absolution, the peace of communion; and those other facts, the existence and potency of human ideals, which, like truth and virtue and beauty, always transcend the concrete and always reveal further goals to the actual. It also includes facts and forces of nature outside and apart from man—the existence of matter and of myriads of other living beings, the position of man on a little planet of one of a million suns, the facts and laws of motion, matter, and energy and all their manifestations, the history of life. I say that it includes these; it would be more correct to say that it includes certain aspects of all these and many other facts. It includes them in their aspect of relatedness to human destiny; and it includes them as held together, against the cosmic background, by a spirit of awe or reverence. If you wish more precision, it includes them in their sacred aspect, or at least in association with an outlook which is reverent or finds holiness in reality.

Finally, it includes them not merely disjointedly, as so many separate items: it includes them in a more or less unified whole, as an organized scheme of thought; and as a matter of fact this scheme tends in its higher manifestations to be organized somewhat after the pattern in which a human personality is organized. It is this, among the other causes that I have mentioned, which helps to give this organized scheme of thought the illusion of possessing personality.

'. . . This, to my mind, is what actually occurs when men speak of communion with God. It is an organising of our experiences of the universe in relation with the driving forces of our soul or mental being, so that the two are united and harmonised' (*Essays of a Biologist*, p. 284). . . .

We may put it in this way. The normal man has an innate capacity for experiencing sanctity in certain events, just as (on a lower and more determinate plane) he has for experiencing red or blue, fear or disgust or desire, or as he has for experiencing beauty, or the validity of logical proof, or for feeling love or hate, or judging good and evil. Some have this in an overmastering degree, and will be haunted all their days by their experiences of holiness and the felt need of conforming their life to them. The majority, on the other hand, have it much less intensely. They will, in their degree, understand holiness when it is pointed out to them, but be incapable of the pioneering discoveries or the power of expression of the exceptional few. These few are like the few creators in the world of poetry or music, the rest are like those who can and do respond to the creation of the poets and musicians and value it, while themselves remaining dumb. Finally, there are undoubtedly some who, either congenitally or through their upbringing, are wholly unable to appreciate what is meant by the sacred or the holy, just as there are a few men who are incapable of appreciating music, a few who are born with defect of the retina leading to colour-blindness, a few who are born imbecile, unable to follow a logical chain of reasoning, a few born moral imbeciles, incapable of appreciating what is meant by right or wrong, and many more in whom upbringing or their own mode of life has deadened or wholly distorted this moral sense.

Not only does the normal man have this capacity for experiencing the sense of the sacred, but he demands its satisfaction. This may come through the services of an organised Church, as is shown by the Russian peasants who in many places insisted on building new churches in place of those that official Bolshevism had destroyed or turned to other uses; or through artistic expression; or though a religiously-felt morality, the necessity of which to some minds has been so finely put in *Romola* by George Eliot that I cannot forbear from quoting: 'The highest sort of happiness often brings so much pain with it, that we can only tell it from pain by its being what we would choose before everything else, because our souls see it is good.'

I use the term 'sense of the sacred' or 'sense of the holy' for want of a better. Had it not been overlain by all sorts of alien and irrelevant ideas, *religious sense* or *sentiment* would have been preferable. . . .

In this chapter I have attempted to advance two main ideas, both largely unfamiliar. One is that the essence of religion springs from man's capacity for awe and reverence, that the objects of religion, however much later rationalised by intellect or moralised by ethics, however fossilised by convention or degraded by superstition or fear, are in origin and essence those things, events, and ideas which arouse the feeling of sacredness. On this point, with the testimony of anthropologists and archbishops to back me, I hope to have convinced my readers.

The other is that the idea of supernatural divine beings, far from being a necessity to any and every religion, is an intellectual rationalisation which was necessary, or at least inevitable, at a certain primitive level of thought and culture; which was then, the crucial assumption once made, worked on by man's intellect and by his ethical sense to give such high conceptions as that of the God of the Hebrews after the Exile, or the God of most modern Christian churches; but which now must be abandoned if further religious progress is to be made. . . .

But if religion is not essentially belief in a God or Gods and obedience to their commands or will, what then is it? It is a way of life, an art like other kinds of living, and an art which must be practiced like other arts if we are to achieve anything good in it.

Religious emotion will always exist, will always demand expression. The ways in which it finds expression may be good or may be bad: or, what seems hardly to have been realised, they may be on the whole good for the individual worshipper but bad for the community. Man's scale of desires and values, his spiritual capacities, dictate the direction of his religion, the goal towards which it aspires; the facts of nature and life dictate the limits within which it may move, the trellis on whose framework those desires and emotions must grow if they are to receive the beams of truth's sun, if they aspire above creeping on the ground. It is our duty to know those outer facts truly and completely, to be willing to face all truth and not try to reject what does not tally with out desires: and it is our duty to realize our own capacities, to know what desires are to be put in command, what desires are to be harnessed to subordinate toil, to place our whole tumultuous life of feeling and will under the joint guidance of reverence and reason.

In so far as we do this, we prevent the man of devout religious feeling from being subordinated to a system which may organise the spirit of religion in opposition to discovery or necessary change, or may discharge its power in cruelty and persecution; and we help religion to help the progress of civilisation. But in so far as we neglect this, we are making man a house divided against itself, and allowing the strong tides of religious feeling to run to waste or to break in and devastate the fruit of man's labour. And the choice is in our own hands.

EPILOGUE

Partners on a Common Quest

IS THERE, THEN, A GULF BETWEEN THE ACADEMIC/HUMANISTIC study of religion and its theological study, which cannot be bridged? To be sure, there are differences between the two disciplines, and these must be kept in mind. Theology concentrates its attention on one religion ("Christian theology" or "Buddhist theology"), whereas the humanistic approach most often combines comparisons with a discussion of religion generally. Theology envisions itself as normative, setting forth what the beliefs of a given religion ought to be, given its foundational documents and history, while the academic study of religion concentrates on describing religions as they are without making value judgments. Theology is about doctrines, beliefs; academic/humanistic scholars investigate all aspects of the religion under consideration. Theology is understood to take place within the "circle of faith": It assumes that the theologian is also a believer, personally committed to a life of faith within that theological tradition. Humanistic/academic scholars make no such assumption. An often-repeated corollary to this is that theology seeks to change attitudes—to strengthen or modify faith commitments—whereas the academic study of religion does not. Theology deals with the ultimate truth claims made by the faith of which it is a part, whereas the academic study of religion usually brackets these claims to absolute truth to facilitate discussing the meaning of such a claim to the individual and the faith community.

Equally important as the differences between the two sorts of disciplines are the situations in which it is imperative that they be kept distinct. The addition of religious studies courses to the curricula of public, tax-supported colleges and universities, for example, requires that such courses be conducted in an atmosphere free of advocacy for one or another religion (or for religion or irreligion, more generally).

With these cautions in mind about the legitimate differences between the two areas of study and the necessity, under certain circumstances, of keeping them scrupulously distinct, we return to the question with which we began: Does this mean that there is an unbridgeable chasm between them? I think not. Historically, at best the two have ignored each other. At worst, theology has berated the academic study of religion for its "lack of faith," while the latter has hurled accusations of "intellectual dishonesty" and "fuzzy thinking" at the former. There have certainly been instances in which scholars who studied religion "from the outside" have fallen headlong into the trap of reductionism, of "explaining away" religion by seeing it as an unfortunate outgrowth of something else, such as economic policies or psychological problems. There have also been instances in which theology erred by being less rigorous than it might and by exempting itself from the canons that usually govern public verifiability, claiming special knowledge that one could know only via faith.

These failures of both to live up to their own potentials need to be laid aside. Perhaps the greatest challenge to both disciplines is effecting a reconciliation between them. Neither can be simply collapsed into the other; both must retain their own characters. But each contains within itself the seeds of a new partnership, an alliance in which both can flourish.

We have seen these seeds in the reading selections contained in this volume. Even Karl Barth, with his overriding concern to protect and glorify the sovereignty of God in the revelation event, must acknowledge that revelation is Revelation to someone. In Barth's understanding, revelation would cease being revelation if no one were to receive it as such, because this would compromise God's absolute control of the process. But in Barth's focus on revelation's "objective pole" (revelation is "there" regardless of who does or does not receive it) there is implied a "subjective pole" (revelation is in principle intended to be received).

On the other side of this chasm are Feuerbach and Freud, for whom religion's ideas of God are reduced to nothing but illusion. For both, however, there is still "something there," a reality that transcends individual human consciousness, that is the foundation upon which the structure of illusion is erected. For Feuerbach it is the human species; for Freud, the wishes and desires for the protecting/judging father we do not consciously acknowledge.

The work of Tillich, on the one hand, and Eliade, on the other, begins to suggest how a bridge might be thrown across the chasm. Tillich lived, thought, and wrote "on the boundary" between faith and secularity. His method of correlation is one example of how he works this perspective out in his theology. His insistence that the "courage to be" that transcends the God of theism is grounded in metaphoric and symbolic language is another. Symbols participate in that to which they point; they are more than simply signs. A traffic light is a sign; a flag is a symbol. Religious symbols point to and participate in that which is ultimate, the Ground of Being itself. By their participation in the realm of sacred reality, religious symbols open up that dimension to human beings. The religious symbol is thus the "locus" where divine and human meet. In religious symbols, there are two elements: the element of ultimacy to which the symbol points and into which it draws us, and the element of finite, contingent experience that serves as the vehicle or carrier of ultimacy. Without this dynamic dialectical union of ultimate with proximate meanings, infinite and finite dimensions, the religious symbol would not exist as symbol.[1] Tillich's theology helps us to see how the "human" and the "divine" elements in theology are always interwoven. In the religious symbol, they become inseparable.

From the other side of the discussion, Mircea Eliade also calls our attention to the close relation between the human and the "sacred" in religious symbols, broadening the discussion to include more than just symbols of Christian faith. There are no purely religious phenomena, nor are there any purely ("merely") human ones. Anything at all, in principle, can become a hierophany, a manifestation of the sacred. Something becomes a hierophany as it points beyond itself to the dimension of the sacred, the ultimate. Religious symbols bring about, as Eliade states, a "permanent solidarity between man and the sacred."[2]

Religion has at least as much to do with the establishment of meaning as with the existence of supernatural beings. Specifically religious meaning is established in and through language as it functions symbolically. As Martin Heidegger suggests, the "naming of the gods" establishes World, makes a coherent whole out of human experience, turns the world (a physical entity with no particular relation to human beings) into the World (a configuration of human meanings in constant give and take with the world).

Thus, the truth of religion can be relocated in light of what has been said about the nature of religious symbolism. Theology and the humanistic/academic study of religion do not have to argue over the existence or nonexistence of God. There is, as phenomenology asserts, "something" intended in any human statement, an "intentional object." In religion this intentional object is that which is perceived by the religious person as "the sacred" or "the ultimate." For Jews and Christians it is expressed by the symbol "God" (and perhaps more so for Christians by the symbol of the Christ). It may also be expressed by other symbols: the Buddha, Nirvana, Shiva the Lord of the Dance, the Tao, humanity itself.

The truth of religion thus becomes, as Paul Ricoeur points out, the truth of religious symbols. This truth is consistent with the phenomenological restraint about making statements about existence itself, is "the fulfillment . . . of the signifying intention" of the symbol itself. And because such symbols exist and function in a variety of total symbol contexts, their intentions can be fulfilled in a number of ways.[3] Each of these various ways can develop its own internal systematic interpretation, guided normatively by what is perceived by the group that has chosen to live by it as its signifying intention. This is the role of theology.

However, because the symbols that convey and make concrete the signifying intentions that re-present (make present again) the sacred dimension always do so by conjoining the sacred with a profoundly human dimension, there need to be ways of better understanding precisely this human element. The disciplines included in the academic study of religion, such as sociology, psychology, philosophy, and phenomenology, are the tools by means of which this understanding is carried forward.

Thus, the two approaches are neither two ships passing in the dark of night, having nothing to do with each other, nor enemies locked in conflict over who has the true claim to disputed territory. They are, rather, partners on a common quest, describing and interpreting the same phenomenon from different points of view. "Inside" (the theologian's stance) and "outside" (the academician's stance) are, after all, dimensions of the *same* entity, relative to the location of the observer.

NOTES

Introduction, Part One
1. The summary that follows is heavily indebted to Frederick J. Streng, *Understanding Religious Life*, 3rd ed. (Belmont, Calif.: Wadsworth Publishing Co., 1985), pp. 11-15.
2. Ibid. pp. 193-94.
3. Ibid., p. 223.
4. Ibid., p. 226.

Chapter 1
1. Emile Durkheim, *The Elementary Forms of the Religious Life*, trans. Joseph Ward Swain (New York: The Free Press, 1965), p. 236.
2. Ibid., p. 462.

Chapter 3
1. Sigmund Freud, *The Future of an Illusion*, trans. and ed. James Strachey (Garden City, N.Y.: Anchor/Doubleday, 1964), p. 24.

Chapter 4
1. Carl G. Jung, *Psychology and Religion: West and East*, 2nd ed., trans. R. F. C. Hull (Princeton, N.J.: Princeton University Press, 1969), p. 845.
2. Carl G. Jung, *Civilization in Transition*, vol. 10 of *The Collected Works of C. G. Jung*, eds. Sir Herbert Read, Michael Fordham, Gerhard Adler (New York: Pantheon Books for the Bollinger Foundation, 1964), p. 395.

Chapter 5
1. Martin Heidegger, *Poetry, Language, Thought*, trans. Albert Hofstadter (New York: Harper & Row, 1971), pp. 150-51.
2. Ibid., p. 117.

Chapter 6
1. Wendell C. Beane and William G. Doty, *Myths, Rites, Symbols: A Mircea Eliade Reader*, vol. 1 (New York: Harper & Row, 1975), pp. xxv-xxvi.

Introduction, Part Two
1. Paul J. Tillich, *Systematic Theology*, vol. 1 (Chicago: University of Chicago Press, 1967), pp. 8-11.
2. John 14:6; Psalm 19:1.

NOTES

3. E. J. Carnell, *The Case for Biblical Christianity*, ed. Ronald H. Nash (Grand Rapids, Mich.: Eerdmans, 1969), pp. 48-49.
4. L. Harold DeWolf, *The Case for Theology in a Liberal Perspective* (Philadelphia: Westminster Press, 1959), pp. 18-19.

Chapter 7
1. Daniel Jenkins, "Karl Barth," in *A Handbook of Christian Theologians*, ed. Dean G. Peerman and Martin E. Marty (Cleveland: World Publishing Co., 1965), p. 396.
2. Heinz Zahrnt, *The Question of God: Protestant Theology in the Twentieth Century*, trans. R. A. Wilson (New York: Harcourt Brace Jovanovich, 1966), pp. 15-16.
3. Jenkins, "Karl Barth," p. 398.
4. Zahrnt, *The Question of God*, p. 89.

Chapter 11
1. W. H. Walsh, "Immanuel Kant," in *Encyclopedia of Philosophy*, vol. 4, ed. Paul Edwards (New York: Macmillan and Free Press, 1967), p. 305.
2. Claude Welch, *Protestant Thought in the Nineteenth Century (1799–1870)*, vol. 1 (New Haven, Conn.: Yale University Press, 1972), p. 45.

Chapter 12
1. Wilhelm Pauck and Marion Pauck, *Paul Tillich: His Life and Thought*, vol. 1, *Life* (New York: Harper & Row, 1976), p. 7.
2. Paul Tillich, *The Shaking of the Foundations* (New York: Charles Scribner's Sons, 1948), p. 57.
3. Charles W. Kegley and Robert W. Bretall, eds., *The Theology of Paul Tillich* (New York: Macmillan, 1964), p. x.
4. Paul Tillich, *Systematic Theology*, vol. 1 (Chicago: University of Chicago Press, 1967), pp. 60-63.
5. Ibid., pp. 64-65.

Chapter 13
1. Friedrich Schleiermacher, *On Religion: Speeches to Its Cultured Despisers* (New York: Harper & Row, 1958), p. 39.
2. Julian Huxley, *Religion Without Revelation* (New York: Harper & Row, 1957), pp. ix-x.

Epilogue
1. Tillich discussed religious symbolism in a variety of contexts. See the following articles and essays, all by Paul Tillich: "Theology and Symbolism," in *Religious Symbolism*, ed. F. Ernest Johnson (New York: Harper and Bros., 1955), pp. 107-16; "The Religious Symbol," in *Symbolism in Religion and Literature*, ed. Rollo May (New York: George Braziller, 1960), pp. 75-98; "Symbols and Faith," chapter 3 of Tillich's *Dynamics of Faith* (New York: Harper & Row, 1957), pp. 41-54; and "The Nature of Religious Language," chapter 5 of Tillich's *Theology of Culture* (London: Oxford University Press, 1959), pp. 53-67.
2. Mircea Eliade, Patterns in Comparative Religion, trans. Rosemary Sheed (New York: Sheed & Ward, 1958), p. 447.
3. Paul Ricoeur, *Freud and Philosophy: An Essay on Interpretation*, trans. Denis Savage (New Haven, Conn.: Yale University Press, 1970), p. 30. In addition to this work, see also his *The Conflict in Interpretations*, ed. Don Ihde (Evanston, Ill.: Northwestern University Press, 1974). Both are excellent philosophical analyses of this issue.